CHURCHILL'S LEGACY

TWO SPEECHES TO SAVE THE WORLD

ALAN WATSON

B L O O M S B U R Y

LONDON · OXFORD · NEW YORK · NEW DELHI · SYDNEY

Bloomsbury Publishing
An imprint of Bloomsbury Publishing Plc

50 Bedford Square
London
WC1B 3DP
UK

1385 Broadway
New York
NY 10018
USA

www.bloomsbury.com

First published in Great Britain 2016

British Library Cataloguing-in-Publication Data
A catalogue record for this book is available from the British Library.

Library of Congress Cataloguing-in-Publication data has been applied for.

ISBN: HB: 978-1-4088-8021-0
ePub: 978-1-4088-8023-4

10 9 8 7 6 5 4 3 2 1

Typeset by Newgen Knowledge Works (P) Ltd., Chennai, India
Printed and bound in Great Britain by CPI Group (UK) Ltd, Croydon CR0 4YY

To find out more about our authors and books visit www.bloomsbury.com.
Here you will find extracts, author interviews, details of forthcoming events and the
option to sign up for our newsletters.

To my wife on our golden wedding anniversary

'An appeaser is one who feeds a crocodile – hoping it will eat him last.'
Winston Churchill

CONTENTS

PART IV

'It hasn't half kicked-up a shindig'

PART V

Europe Restored

PART VI

Winners and Losers

FOREWORD BY RANDOLPH CHURCHILL

Sir Winston Churchill's leadership in the Second World War is well documented. Of all the years of my great-grandfather's life, 1940 is often seen as the most decisive. His stand against Hitler kept Britain in the conflict and made the liberation of Western Europe possible. But at the end of the war that hard-won liberty seemed threatened anew. *Churchill's Legacy: Two Speeches to Change the World* argues for a wider perspective and makes a powerful case for an equally decisive year – 1946.

The Europe of 1946 was devastated by war. Churchill was at a low point in his political career. Rejected by the British electorate, his wife, Clementine, consoled him by saying, 'It may well be a blessing in disguise.' Churchill replied, 'At the moment it seems quite effectively disguised.'[1]

Penetrating this gloom was a letter inviting him to travel to an obscure college at Fulton, Missouri, with a galvanising footnote from Truman promising to accompany him if he accepted. Having travelled to Fulton with the president, Churchill delivered his 'Iron Curtain' speech warning of the danger to the West posed by Soviet hegemony over Central and Eastern Europe, and Soviet ambition for even more power. Churchill said that this was the most important speech he had ever made.

Nineteen forty-six was becoming, for Churchill, as important as 1940. The foe had changed but the threat was comparable. He argued for a US commitment to defend Europe – a commitment that had not been made in 1940 when Britain stood alone.

The Roosevelt family was appalled. The US media and much of American public opinion denigrated Churchill as a warmonger intent on a crusade against 'good old Uncle Joe'. Truman backed away, denying that his presence at Fulton was any kind of endorsement and even claiming – quite wrongly – that he did not know what Churchill was going to say.

This is a tale that has been told before, although never with the detail, political awareness and documentary evidence drawn from the Churchill Archives at Cambridge that empower the narrative of *Churchill's Legacy*. Lord Alan Watson analyses the causes and consequences that link Fulton with Churchill's second speech of 1946, delivered six months later in Zurich on 19 September, and explains how they work together to create a vision for confronting communism.

It is easy today for us, the younger generation that has not known the horrors of world war, to take for granted our freedoms and liberties. However, at the end of the Second World War Churchill realised that communist Russia and its ruthless, murdering dictator Joseph Stalin posed an immense threat to European stability. Europe was weak and bankrupt: Russia, the big bear, stood in an aggressive and dominating position. Hitler was beaten and people assumed the war was won. Yet the Russian bear was in the heart of the great capitals of Europe. After the First World War, Churchill continuously sought to strengthen the League of Nations which the Americans abandoned. In 1946 he saw again that without the backing of America to defend freedom in Europe we might be thrown into a further world war made more grievous in a new atomic age. At Fulton, Churchill appealed to the United States as the world's only nuclear power to defend Europe. The atomic bomb coupled with their financial dominance gave them the means and the opportunity to do so.

But Churchill knew that if this commitment was not matched by an internal commitment to revitalise and repair the shattered economy and political stability of Europe, then Western Europe could still fall. Churchill's genius in his second speech was to understand the American position and to shock Europe into action that would win the commitment of the USA – economically and politically.

Churchill called for a kind of 'United States of Europe' led by France and Germany. Only their reconciliation would restore France's 'moral leadership' and there would be 'no revival of Europe without a spiritually great France and a spiritually great Germany'. Churchill's challenge to the status quo of recrimination and despair equalled that of Fulton. Initially it was also rejected. The Nuremberg trials made the idea of reconciliation repugnant to most at a time when the full extent of Nazi atrocities was being revealed.

Still Churchill was haunted by the blindness that had led to 1940 and his failure to get the world to listen before it was too late. In 1946 he got the world to listen. The scale and insight of his vision in making these two speeches has never been truly understood and never adequately explained.

To Churchill's relief and profound satisfaction, both speeches succeeded. Truman enunciated the Truman Doctrine, committing America to defend freedom. He wrote to Churchill in 1947: 'Your Fulton speech becomes more nearly a prophecy every day.'[2]

In the same year George C. Marshall inaugurated the Marshall Plan to restore Europe's economy. Churchill quoted with great satisfaction Marshall's acknowledgement that his plan was 'directly linked' with the declarations and proposals for the Union of Europe which he had revived in Zurich.

The West defied Stalin's blockade of Berlin a year later. The shape and direction of the world was altered. *Churchill's Legacy* tells how and why Churchill achieved this. Lord Watson contributes a vital dimension to our understanding of Churchill and his vision.

He superbly sheds light on the two remarkable and insightful speeches, which in 1946 helped to save the world. They did so by ensuring the United States played their full part in defending the cherished European liberties, but that America also played her full part in the rebuilding and recovery of Europe.

It is heartening that at the place where Churchill gave that great address at Fulton in the Midwest, the Trustees of Westminster College in the early 1960s sought a way to commemorate it. Shortly thereafter they acquired St Mary Aldermanbury, a beautiful City of London church designed by Sir Christopher Wren, which had been flattened by the Luftwaffe during the Battle of Britain. In tribute to Churchill they rebuilt it lovingly, stone by stone, at Fulton and underneath they created the remarkable National Churchill Museum. After the fall of the Berlin Wall in 1989, the greatest political event of my lifetime, Churchill's granddaughter, the artist Edwina Sandys, was inspired to acquire several sections of the wall. Using them, she sculpted *Breakthrough* encapsulating the idea that the human spirit always seeks freedom and liberty and will not be denied. This historic piece stands beside the National Churchill Museum.

I grew up in the Cold War, in a world divided by the Iron Curtain, but in a West that was protected by the shield of the trans-Atlantic and European alliances that were forged in that immediate post-war era, and that were first articulated by my great-grandfather seventy years ago in those two monumental speeches of 1946.

Lord Watson's book is a fine and perceptive tribute to my great-grandfather's political instincts and his courageous approach to difficult international matters. It also acts as a reminder of the need of vigilance and tenacity in defence of our hard-won freedoms.

Although Churchill died fifty years ago the foundations to our current peace and freedom are drawn from those two speeches of 1946. Let us never forget the brave men and women who fought and gave their lives to secure us those liberties.

ABBREVIATIONS

BBC	British Broadcasting Corporation
CAC	Churchill Archives Centre
FCO	Foreign and Commonwealth Office
ISIS	Islamic State of Iraq and Syria
MP	Member of Parliament
NATO	North Atlantic Treaty Organisation
OM	Order of Merit
RAF	Royal Air Force
UK	United Kingdom
UN	United Nations
UNESCO	United Nations Educational, Scientific and Cultural Organisation
USA	United States of America
USS	United States Ship
USSR	Union of Soviet Socialist Republics

Introduction

This book is about Sir Winston Churchill's second endeavour to save the freedom of the world. His first was in 1940, when he had led Britain's defiance of tyranny, enabling eventual victory. Defeat in the Battle of Britain and Nazi occupation would have precluded US intervention against Hitler and ultimately condemned Europe to either total German occupation or total Soviet domination.

Six years later, Churchill's imperative was to frustrate a new tyranny by winning the support of the United States in the restoration of Europe. This meant defending Europe and restoring its economic life. Both would prove impossible without the total commitment of the United States, its government and its people. To this end, Churchill focused all his energies in 1946.

Churchill's visit to the United States at the beginning of the year was crucial. He alone had the status and audacity to reveal Stalin for what he was – a tyrant determined to dominate Europe at any cost, except nuclear war. The controversy he ignited also had the effect of restoring his morale, and enabling him to shake off a depression that had gripped him since his electoral defeat the previous year.

His vision of how to preserve freedom required a further initiative. In September 1946 he gave his second speech to save the world, this time in Zurich, Switzerland. It astonished his audience, for he proposed nothing less than a partnership between France and Germany, an idea that he knew was anathema to the French. However, as at Fulton, he warned that time might be short.

To understand what Churchill intended with these two speeches requires perspective. The daring of his imagination and the scale of his architecture for a new Western alliance was extraordinary. At the time, not many recognised the symmetry of what he proposed.

At Churchill's funeral in 1965, commentators bemoaned the end of an era. In truth, Churchill was the catalyst of a new era – one built upon effective defence, economic revival and European unity.

PART I

RUSSIAN MENACE,
WESTERN WEAKNESS

I

The Warnings

Churchill loathed Bolshevism. He did so from its inception. He did not live to witness its demise but his boldness in 1946 contributed decisively to its containment, the frustration of Stalin's aggression and the eventual implosion of the Soviet empire.

His attitude towards Russia and its people was complex. In 1919 he backed military intervention in their civil war. After the Bolshevik victory he pitied the Russians as 'a people ruled by terror, fanaticism and the secret police'.[1] He admired their extraordinary courage following the Nazi invasion of the Soviet Union and acknowledged the free world's debt to them. 'I have always believed that it is the Red Army that has torn the guts out of the filthy Nazis,' he proclaimed in a toast to Stalin in the Kremlin in 1944.[2] He hoped, against the evidence, that a settlement with Stalin might be reached eventually. However, for him the basic character of Bolshevism was malignant. 'Trying to maintain good relations with a communist is like wooing a crocodile. You do not know whether to tickle it under the chin or to beat it over the head. When it opens its mouth you cannot tell whether it is trying to smile or preparing to eat you up.'[3]

In 1946 Churchill knew that the moment had come to hit it over the head. To do that he had to persuade the United States to change its attitude to Stalin and the USSR. It was time for his crusade to America.

In the USA Stalin was still seen by most as 'good old Uncle Joe', the wartime ally persistently wooed by President Franklin D. Roosevelt whose inherent dislike of British imperialism exceeded his suspicion of Soviet ambition. Could American sentiment be turned? There were some who hoped so – to an extent – including Roosevelt's successor Harry S. Truman. But only to a calculated degree.

To those both in London and Washington who sensed the growing danger of Soviet power there was a recognition that if anyone was to sound the alarm it had better be Churchill. It was worth the gamble, but a gamble it was.

Churchill was no longer prime minister. He had been comprehensively beaten in the 1945 general election by Clement Attlee and the Labour Party. With Churchill igno-miniously ousted from the Potsdam victors' conference in Berlin in 1945, his chair taken by Attlee, Churchill now faced political oblivion. Leading the Conservative Party in opposi-tion was not a task he relished. He and his party did not much like each other and Churchill was demoralised. He expressed his anguish with candour in the concluding pages of his book *The Second World War:* 'All the pressure of great events, on and against which I had mentally so long maintained my "flying speed", would cease and I should fall.'[4]

Defeated and disheartened, would he still have the status and appetite to launch a crusade to alert the USA to the imperative of resisting Stalin's appetite for total hegemony in Europe? Could he alert the United States before it was too late? After all, previous warnings had not led to effective action.

In fact, by the end of the Second World War in Europe it was abundantly clear that Stalin's ambition was not limited to the defeat of Nazi Germany. He was intent on establishing Soviet rule wherever the Red Army was in place. Before taking Berlin he told his inner circle, 'This war is not as in the past. Whoever occupies a territory also imposes on it his own social system – as far as his army can reach.'[5] In doing this he discarded the pledge he had given Churchill and Roosevelt at Yalta that the liberated peoples of Eastern Europe would be able to create democratic institutions of their own choice. By 1946 Winston Churchill believed that only the USA, fully committed alongside Britain, could prevent Stalin extending his power even beyond the demarcations agreed at Potsdam, the concluding Allied conference.

Churchill saw menace. He confided to Canada's prime minister, Mackenzie King, that all Berlin would be on Stalin's list – not merely the Soviet sector. He was alarmed by Russian intransigence over Iran. Above all he was appalled by the speed and scale of the repatriation of US troops, denuding Western Europe's defence in front of the mass formations of the Red Army.

It would take Churchill's crusade to the USA in early 1946 to fully alert American opinion, but the warnings had been accumulating for years.

The most prescient came in October 1942 when German Panzers were less than 100 km from Moscow. Britain's third secretary at its Moscow embassy reported to London:

One of my nightmares is that if the Russian armies are eventually successful as I think they will be, they will end this war by marching to Berlin and occupying all points of Europe east. And then how are we going to get them out? There is going to be a most unholy row between us when this thing is over. The final atmosphere of suspicion and mistrust will be far worse than it was two or three years ago [i.e. the time of the Stalin–Ribbentrop pact].[6]

The most ferocious and comprehensive warning came from another diplomat over three years later. George Kennan was the number two at the American embassy in Moscow. His 'long telegram' arrived in Washington on 22 February 1946, two weeks before Churchill's speech at Fulton. It was secret but caused a sensation in the US administration. It advocated a policy of containment. He believed Roosevelt's attitude to Stalin had amounted to appeasement especially at the first 'Big Three' conference at Tehran. Roosevelt had demonstrated his belief that if only Stalin 'could be exposed to the persuasive charms of someone like Roosevelt himself . . . Stalin's co-operation with the West could easily be arranged'. Kennan concluded that 'for these assumptions there were no grounds whatever and they were of a puerility unworthy of Roosevelt's status'.[7]

The third warning also came from a diplomat, this time British. Sir Frank Roberts joined the diplomatic service in 1930 and was Britain's negotiator in Moscow on the Berlin blockade. Later he served as ambassador to NATO, the USSR and the Federal Republic of Germany. Interviewed by me for BBC Radio 4, he described the 'long dispatches' sent by him to London in February 1946. He and Kennan consulted each other. Their conclusions were 'very close', although Roberts had an inevitable British preoccupation with Soviet influence and propaganda in the British Empire that might disrupt the gradual and peaceful termination of imperial rule and its transformation to the equality of the Commonwealth. He and Kennan agreed on a policy of firm containment, which would deter Russia from a war she feared.

Roberts had the good fortune to report to Ernest Bevin, the Labour government's formidable foreign secretary whose experience of dealing with communism in the British trade unions made him wily and forceful. The Berlin airlift would not have happened without him just as it could not have been attempted without the impact of Churchill's crusade to alert the West to the dangers it faced.[8]

What was ultimately at stake was spelled out by the British Foreign Office at the very start of Stalin's blockade of that city. The FCO stated:

> If the Soviet Government were to succeed in their efforts to force us out of Berlin, the effect would be extremely grave not only in Berlin but in Western Germany and in Europe at large. It might prove impossible for the Western powers to maintain their position at all in Western Germany if Berlin were lost to them except by heavily reinforcing the military forces there.[9]

Sir Frank Roberts confirmed to me many times that this was Bevin's personal conviction. It was unequivocally Churchill's conviction as expressed in his speech in the House of Commons in June 1948. He followed Bevin in the debate on Berlin saying 'there can be no doubt that the communist government of Russia has made up its mind to drive us and France and all the other allies out and turn the Russian zone in Germany into one of the satellite states under the rule of totalitarian terrorism'.[10] It was because the threat was so grave that the Truman administration authorised the stationing of two B29 bomber groups in Britain during the Berlin crisis. Thus, subsequent events fully justified Churchill's 1946 crusade.

Churchill and Roosevelt

The relationship between Churchill and Roosevelt was a court-ship without consummation. On Churchill's side it was pursued initially with calculation and determination. There was no other choice. He drew not just from the wells of necessity but also from the depths of affection and affinity so real to him. He loved, admired and gained energy from America. Had his father, not his mother, been American he might have achieved the White House himself. He teased Congress with this thought but also teased himself. However, courtships are not without pain and Roosevelt placed daggers in Churchill's heart. This chapter describes a rela-tionship that ultimately and intimately failed and jeopardised the West.

The seeds of this misfortune were sown early – long before there was any relationship between the two men. Only months after his election as president in March 1933, Roosevelt had revoked America's post-revolutionary hostility to the USSR. That November he established diplomatic relations between the two nations, signing the official agreement with the Soviet Union's foreign minister, Maxim Litvinov.

William Bullitt became the USA's first ambassador to Moscow. Bullitt had a background of some privilege. He was from a wealthy Philadelphian family and was educated at Yale. It was a background that appealed to Roosevelt. He also had a track record at the State Department where he had long argued for the diplomatic recognition of the USSR which, like the president, he saw as 'a promising experiment in a new form of government'.[1]

Events in Moscow had persuaded him that Stalin was a tyrant, only too willing and able to rule by terror. Bullitt was sickened by Stalin's mass arrests, and the show trials preceded by torture, extracting the confessions which then made execution inevitable. Bullitt was realistic. For him, the honeymoon was over.

However Roosevelt 'clung to the notion that the Soviet Union would eventually develop more democratic institutions and abandon its aggressive notions of spreading communism elsewhere'.[2] In 1936, the Roosevelt administration replaced Bullitt with Joseph Davies, a friend of the president's and a generous contributor to his campaign funds. Unlike Bullitt, he was not in the least dismayed by the Moscow show trials. Indeed he reported that, like most diplomats in the Soviet capital, he believed 'the accused must have been guilty of an offense which in the Soviet Union would merit the death penalty' and that consequently 'the Stalin regime politically and internally is probably stronger than heretofore'.[3]

When this proved not to be the case in 1941, as the German armies swept into the Soviet Union, Davies was unrepentant. He now had a fresh imperative – to urge the greatest possible flow of Allied aid to the embattled Russians. Here he was more realistic, recognising that Soviet resistance was toughening all the time and the winter could well save Moscow.

That aid to Russia was vital, and Churchill was as committed to it as Roosevelt. But their approach was different. The Arctic convoys tested and demonstrated British courage and commitment, but Churchill never viewed Russia as an ally worthy of unconditional support. The absolute priority was to defeat Hitler and that made Stalin an ally, but not a friend. Bolshevism precluded that; for Churchill, the warnings of Stalin's menace were writ large on the battlefields and in the summits that concluded the war.

A crucial development for Churchill, both in his detestation of Stalin's callousness and his growing frustration with Roosevelt, occurred in late July 1944. The Red Army was near to Warsaw. Radio Moscow appealed to the Warsaw Home Army to rise against the Nazis. They did, but instead of coming to their aid the Soviets halted on the Vistula. Some have argued that this was simply because 'the Russian offensive has reached the end of its tether' for the time being. Alan Clark, in *Barbarossa*, accepts this but also admits that once Stalin judged that the Polish Home Army 'had shot its bolt', he ordered the communist-led Polish force under Soviet control 'to enter the battle and fight their way into Warsaw'.[4]

What cannot be doubted is that Stalin's priority was to ensure Warsaw's submission to 'his' Poles, and this was the outcome. The rising by the Polish Home Army, and with it all hope of a Polish democracy, was eradicated by the SS with no attempt by the Soviets to halt the massacre.

The rising was therefore wiped out, and the Poles killed or sent to camps. Churchill had implored Stalin to allow Allied aircraft to land, refuel and supply the Poles from Soviet-controlled airfields. He wrote to Stalin, 'Unless you directly forbid it, we propose to send the planes.' But Roosevelt would not endorse or join the appeal. 'I do not consider it advantageous for me to join with you in [your] proposed message to Uncle Joe.' Stalin had shown his hand but so too had Roosevelt. He was unwilling to offend Stalin who he believed could be won over by Western concessions.[5]

This combination of outrage with Stalin and disappointment with Roosevelt proved toxic. Churchill was unwilling to accept the accumulating evidence of both Soviet ruthlessness and presidential weakness. In his *The Second World War*, Churchill sought to play down the widening divergence between the UK and USA over the Soviet Union. It embarrassed him then and later but also energised his crusade. Roosevelt's concessions to Stalin at Tehran, his slighting of Churchill at Yalta, his ceaseless attempts to parley privately with Stalin, all compounded the prime minister's frustration and resentment. It may well have contributed to his decision not to attend Roosevelt's funeral in Washington and certainly motivated him to grasp the opportunity to travel to Fulton with President Truman. The Anglo-American rift had to be bridged if Stalin was to be contained.

What was Roosevelt's motivation in all this? In 1941 on the battleship *Prince of Wales*, when Churchill and Roosevelt met in Argentia Bay, Roosevelt shared much of his motivation with his son Elliot.[6] Elliot recorded that Roosevelt had a visceral distrust of British imperialism and of Churchill whom he saw as its embodiment. Churchill was hurt, offended and enraged by Roosevelt's unwarranted strictures on India and alarmed by his vulnerability to Stalin. But his wooing of Roosevelt was as imperative as Roosevelt's wooing of Stalin was compulsive.

The tension in the relationship between the two Western allies vis-à-vis the Soviet Union was not restricted to the wartime conferences although Churchill's unhappiness over Poland at Yalta must have been abundantly evident to Roosevelt. The president's preference for one-on-one meetings between Stalin and himself demonstrated the divergence of approach that so strained his relationship with Churchill.

The differences were also evidenced on the battlefields as the war reached its conclusion, and they were not only between Churchill and Roosevelt. Others were also involved at the highest level. Churchill got on well with Eisenhower, preferring his diplomatic skill and emollient style to the waspish behaviour of his own top commander, Montgomery, whom he described as 'indomitable in retreat, invincible in advance, insufferable in victory'.[7]

Nevertheless, Churchill wanted one key victory from Montgomery in the final days of the war and he wanted it even at the risk of deeply upsetting Roosevelt and infuriating Stalin. Churchill was determined that the Soviets be denied the capture of Denmark from the Germans. With the Red Army poised to sweep on down the Baltics he was delighted with Montgomery's theatrical and opportunistic triumph on Lüneburg Heath on 3 May 1945 and the extraordinary bravado of Monty's troops in the days following.

Monty's mobile headquarters – essentially a hub of caravans surrounded by constant activity – was to be the setting for a German surrender that the field marshal and the prime minister wanted to be seen as *the* German surrender, delivering to the British nearly a quarter of a million German troops including all of those in Holland, Schleswig-Holstein and Denmark.[8]

When the German delegation arrived at 11.30am on 3 May, led by Admiral von Friedeburg, who by then headed up what remained of Dönitz's navy, it also included Field Marshal Busch's chief of staff. Busch commanded the Wehrmacht's North West Army Group, desperate to be captured by the British and not the Russians. In fact, the admiral was carrying a letter offering to surrender all the German forces facing the Russians between Berlin and Rostock. It was a dramatic if understandable move. With Hitler having committed suicide in Berlin at the end of April and the Soviets occupying the capital, what was the point of the three German armies involved resisting the British? Montgomery held to the Allied agreement. These German armies must surrender to the Russians. 'Unthinkable,' blustered von Friedeburg. Monty's reply was razor sharp: 'I said that the Germans should have thought of all these things before they began the war, and particularly before they attacked the Russians.'[9]

But then without a pause Montgomery asked von Friedeburg, 'Will you surrender all German forces on my western and northern flanks, including all forces in Holland, Schleswig-Holstein, and Denmark?' Von Friedeburg left to report to Dönitz, Hitler's nominated successor. The next afternoon he returned and, after keeping the Germans waiting for half an hour, Montgomery accepted his surrender.

It was a triumph. Montgomery's armies had already occupied Lübeck and Wismar. On 5 May they arrived in Kiel. The next day they liberated Holland. Within days they had freed Copenhagen. It was a stunning achievement but it threw down a gauntlet in front of Stalin. The British had pushed sixty miles across the truce line negotiated with the Russians. Eisenhower was annoyed and alarmed. A victory on this scale was 'outside Montgomery's remit'.[10] The surrender of Denmark could only take place with Russian representatives. None were invited to Lüneburg Heath. Churchill, who did not in the least share Eisenhower's trust in Russian assurances, was convinced they planned to take Copenhagen. He backed Montgomery and, with great reluctance, Eisenhower accepted the fait accompli.

The high drama of the closing days of the war, with its exhilarating evidence of a significant British victory and the defiance of Stalin, could not compensate Churchill for what then happened at the war's last Allied summit – at Potsdam outside Berlin. An Iron Curtain was indeed falling over Eastern Europe and America's successful testing of its atomic bomb could not reverse the Soviet Union's occupation on the ground of Eastern Europe. The USSR

saw all the lands occupied by the Red Army as destined ultimately
to be controlled by Moscow using all the apparatus of the totalitarian Communist Party being installed country by country. The
phrase 'Iron Curtain' was not in itself original, having been coined
by Joseph Goebbels. The process was intended to be irreversible
where the Red Army had conquered. But if Russia was not to
advance further they could not be stopped by the sort of *coup de
théâtre* engineered by Montgomery in 1945. What was needed was
a new Allied strategy – a bold and radical restructuring of the
Atlantic Alliance.

Could Churchill be given the chance to play any role in this
new act of political creation? The British electorate had rejected
him. His 'black-dog' mood threatened to extinguish his
resolution.

Fortunately he remained determined to woo the USA and its
president in Britain's interest and that of the free world. After
Potsdam and the British general election it seemed unlikely that
the opportunity would occur, but it did.

3

Berlin 1945

The courtship of Roosevelt's successor was not on Churchill's agenda when he met Truman in Berlin for the Allies' concluding conference of the war. His preoccupation was to seek and, even at this late hour, wrest some concession from Stalin over Poland. Churchill knew what was happening behind the Iron Curtain. When he deployed that phrase with such effect on his American crusade it would cause a sensation – as would his assertion that behind that ruthless division of a continent terrible things were afoot. In truth Churchill, in Berlin, already had a pretty good idea of what was happening. In Poland, and in every country the Red Army had conquered, the USSR was putting in place the essentials of Soviet control. Politicians, often nurtured in wartime Moscow and others approved by the Kremlin, were being positioned for absolute power. Opponents of the Party were being arrested. As Stalin had explained to his aides his social and political system would have an absolute monopoly of control. This was the reality. The promises he had given previously at the Yalta Conference were fiction. There would be no free elections. The people he had conquered would have no more choice of who their rulers would be than the peoples of the Soviet Union.

The conference in the Cecilienhof was to yield two surprises. It was an odd setting – a rambling, country get-away palace built

in the English Edwardian style for the Kaiser's family during the
First World War. Its rooms were allocated to the three leaders and
their staff. The main hall, later immortalised by the many photographs taken, was dominated by a large circular table and the three
great chairs in which Stalin, Churchill and Truman took their
places as the 'Big Three'.

In the 1960s, when I made the BBC's first documentary on the
German Democratic Republic (DDR), I sat in Stalin's chair to
record a piece to camera. It was late and dark outside. I was nervous
and had to record the piece several times. The East German offi-
cials and minders were far more nervous. What was happening in
the pool of light thrown on the scene by the BBC's technicians
was dangerous – an Englishman, the first since Churchill and
Attlee, expressing his views across this table and sitting in Stalin's
chair. In the silence, while we were waiting to record, a phone
rang from the gloom in one corner of the room. Everyone jumped.
It was as if the ghost had chosen to halt the sacrilege. I finished the
piece: 'I am sitting in Stalin's chair, the very seat from which he
witnessed the triumph of his post-war ordering of East and
Central Europe. Neither Britain nor America could prevent this.'

And so it had been, but all was not quite as Stalin expected in
Berlin in 1945. Early in the conference Churchill had left – recalled
to Britain to await the electorate's verdict. Democracy was to be
stifled wherever the Red Army had conquered, but in Britain the
votes of its troops hugely swelled the electorate's rejection of
Churchill. He feared the worst and experienced the most trau-
matic, demoralising defeat of his political life. Stalin must have
found it curious. He did not expect it.

The other surprise – but he may have anticipated it – came just
before Churchill's departure. During a break in the conference
proceedings Truman told Stalin that in the Nevada desert the

Americans had just successfully tested a new bomb of awesome power. He did not say that this weapon could end the war with Japan, thus nullifying Stalin's ambition to become an occupying power in post-war Japan. Even less did Truman indicate that the atomic bomb might prove the countervailing force in a Europe otherwise dominated by the vast superiority of the Red Army. Truman was characteristically modest and brief. Churchill observed the exchange closely. Stalin showed no surprise, simply murmuring his pleasure that such a weapon was now available. In truth he well knew of the possibility if not the timing. His spies embedded in the Manhattan Project had kept him informed.

Thus Potsdam was not entirely predictable. Churchill had gone. The Bomb had arrived. A new era was beginning – one later to be named the 'Cold War'.

Its first real test would follow three years later as Stalin attempted to squeeze the Allies out of Berlin and incorporate their sector of the city. His blockade of Berlin and the breaking of it by an unprecedented airlift led by the United States Air Force and the Royal Air Force was to prove decisive. Stalin was unable to prevent the creation of a free Federal Republic of Germany and its economic recovery symbolised by its new currency, the Deutschmark. From then on Stalin would have to react to a reshaping of Western Europe rather than determine it.

Yet for this to occur, American and indeed British public opinion had to be alerted to the Soviet threat. For containment to be acceptable 'good old Uncle Joe' had to be seen for what he was. In July 1945 that seemed unlikely.

PART II
CHURCHILL'S CHANCE

4

Genesis of the Journey

Churchill's decision to travel to Fulton and make a speech was triggered by an invitation from the president of Westminster College, with a footnote written by hand from the president of the United States. How did both the letter and footnote come to be written?

First the trigger. The Westminster College president, F. L. McCluer, dates his letter 3 October 1945. Truman's footnote is not separately dated:

> Dear Winnie,
> This is a fine old school out in my state. If you come and make a speech there, I'll introduce you.

At the time Winston was receiving many such invitations, and this from a small Midwestern college was brought to his attention only because of Truman's footnote. How did this come to be penned by the president? The author of the letter, McCluer, was a formidable networker. The key man was Truman's military aide, General Harry H. Vaughan, a Westminster alumnus whose assistance McCluer had secured. The letter of invitation was placed before Truman who appended the crucial footnote, 'I'll introduce you'.[1] Churchill will have checked the logistics of this and realised that he would be with Truman on an eighteen-hour train journey.

Churchill was being offered intimate access to the leader of the Western world and therefore was fully motivated.[2]

He replied:

> If you, as you suggest in your postscript, would like me to visit your home State and would introduce me, I should feel it my duty – and it would be a great pleasure – to deliver an address to the Westminster University on the world situation, under your aegis. This might possibly be advantageous from several points of view.[3]

Churchill would insist, before and after the Fulton speech, that he was speaking in a private capacity but he clearly trusted that Truman would be there as president, publicly seen to endorse what he would propose. Indeed the film coverage shows Truman enthusiastically applauding the crucial sections of the speech – not only the warning of the Iron Curtain but also the British–American alliance to counter the Soviet threat.

The advocacy of this alliance was Churchill's predominant political motive in accepting the invitation. He would headline it as 'the crux of what I have travelled here to say'. There is background to this sense of priority. It was his experience of the price paid for appeasement (a term he would use in the Fulton speech) and equally the cost of inaction in opposing Hitler.

One of his most famous and successful pre-Second World War speeches was in the House of Commons on 12 November 1936. He castigated Baldwin's government for being 'decided only to be undecided, resolved to be irresolute, adamant for drift'. He was appalled by this paralysis in the face of the growing threat.[4] These were 'the years that the locust hath eaten'.[5] He was determined to avoid a repeat of the locust years.

Churchill was haunted by a nightmare: he had not been heard. He had been unable to break through the barriers of complacency and fear. His lion's roar was muffled – his shout was stifled. At Fulton he relived the frustration of this stasis. He was to recall with anguish, not self-congratulation:

> Last time I saw it coming and cried aloud to my own fellow countrymen and to the world but no one paid any attention . . . but no one could listen and one by one we were all sucked into the awful whirlpool.[6]

Above all he was seized by his sense of urgency. He believed that as before, when he had foreseen the mortal threat posed by Adolf Hitler, the democracies were facing an equal danger from Joseph Stalin. In her autobiography his daughter, Mary, recalled what it was like in 1939:

> On looking back, the late spring and early summer of 1939 seem to stand out with an almost three-dimensional clarity. We were on a countdown . . . During these increasingly fraught months, Winston would often recite a verse he had gleaned as a schoolboy . . . from a volume of Punch cartoons that he had seen at Brighton. The poem had been inspired by a recent railway accident caused by the train driver falling asleep:

> > Who is in charge of the clattering train?
> > For the carriages sway and the couplings strain,
> > And the pace is fast,
> > And the points are near,
> > And sleep had deadened the driver's ear.
> > And the signals flash through the night in vain
> > For DEATH is in charge of the clattering train.
> >
> > Edwin J. Milliken[7]

Churchill's purpose in America was to wrest control of events from death once more, seemingly 'in charge of the clattering train'.

If this was the imperative that drove him – the need to force the world to listen – were there other, very human motivations as well?

He needed to recuperate, not so much from exhaustion after his wartime leadership as from his rejection by British voters afterwards. His 'black-dog' mood had him in its thrall. He needed sun and luxury and he had already accepted an invitation to holiday in Miami for a week at the home of the Canadian Frank Clarke. Clarke was the man to whom, on the train back from Fulton, Churchill confided his verdict that this had been his most important speech. To his doctor, Winston had also confided at the moment when he was voted out of office in 1945 that he feared above all that the power to shape the future would be 'denied me'.[8] Miami was the holiday he needed and the United States the platform he required.

As a younger man he had reflected that 'we are so often mocked by the failures of our hopes'. He felt now to be mocked by fate and the sun of Florida was not enough to dissipate his gloom. He yearned to be again at the centre of great events. He needed to restore his celebrity status. He sensed that in the United States 'they will take things from me'.[9] The prospect of voyaging across the Atlantic to meet the president and capture the headlines, the chance once again to 'grasp the hem of history', was irresistible. Mary, his daughter, was in no doubt. She wrote to him and her mother Clementine, who would travel with him, 'I shall rejoice to imagine you both tossed by star-spangled waves'.[10] This would be a journey to change him and the world.

5

'I am deserted'

It is important not to underestimate what a colossal task these two changes involved. To change Churchill's morale and self-esteem meant repairing the significant, some thought permanent, damage done by defeat and apparent exclusion. The second – changing the world into a safer and more hopeful place after catastrophic global conflict – seemed way beyond the reach of any one mortal, let alone a defeated prime minister.

The physiology and psychology of Churchill in 1945 were tested to near breaking point. In August that year Churchill confessed to his doctor, Lord Moran, something of his real desperation. 'It's no use pretending,' he said, 'I'm not hard hit. I cannot school myself to doing nothing for the rest of my life. It would have been better to have been killed in an aeroplane or to have died like Roosevelt.'[1] To have contemplated death this way and talked about it tells us how fundamental his doubts were about his ability to cope. He desperately needed the adrenalin he and his family hoped would flow into him on his American journey.

Churchill was physically brave. Indeed as a young man he was almost oblivious to danger. Had the Nazis reached London, he would, by instinct, have sought a hero's death, revolver in hand as he depicted himself facing danger in *My Early Life*.[2] That would surely have been his preference had events allowed it. But such admirable spirit could not disguise his sense of physical vulnerability to illness. He was an anxious patient detailing the symptoms that alarmed him, seeking reassurance from Lord Moran throughout the war and after it. He drove himself through the barriers of illness time and time again. Desperately ill before the Tehran Conference, struck down at critical times by influenza, bronchitis, pneumonia and strokes, he battled on. Cigars, whisky, his predilection to be easily but only satisfied with the best, the flamboyance of his clothes from dressing gowns and boiler suits to full dress uniforms, all projected a robustness he did not have or feel. Photographs reveal the cost of survival.[3] Physical vulnerability and anxiety, for Churchill, were interconnected. One often led to the other and even though he resolutely overcame illness in order to stay on top of events, his frequent but temporary corporal weaknesses fed into his character-istic bouts of depression and vice versa.

There was another corrosive force impairing his self-confidence. Not only defeated at the polls in 1945, he knew he had never won Downing Street by election. Somewhat reluctantly he had been chosen by the king and his own party for the highest office in 1940, but only the depth of the national crisis produced his elevation. With the war over, he was rejected. Did he have the energy and will to win the premiership for himself? If Churchill had been sure in August 1945, he would not have contemplated doing 'nothing for the rest of my life'.[4] Like Truman, who took the Oval Office on the death of Roosevelt and not on the vote of the electorate, he felt that he had to win power at the polls for himself. In the case of Truman, this would involve a very tough election in 1948 but he had no doubt that he could do it. In the case of Churchill, he had not determined to run until after the stimulus of his US visit.

Electoral defeat and exclusion from the top table at Potsdam marked the nadir of decline already evident before the war's end.

Alexander Cadogan's diaries record the concerns of Churchill's inner circle. On 19 April 1944, Cadogan confided to his diary after a particularly frustrating cabinet meeting: 'P.M. I fear is breaking down. He rambles without a pause. I am really fussed about the P.M. He is not the man he was 12 months ago and I really don't know whether he can carry on . . .'[5]

What is important in Cadogan's entry is that it goes beyond irritation. It expresses real anxiety. Of course Churchill's habits and ways of working had exasperated many during the war years. So often sharp and witty he could also be loquacious and repetitive. He was consistently selfish about other people's timetables – sleeping for quite long 'siestas' during the afternoon and requiring attendance and attention in the early hours of the morning. Sometimes brusque, often argumentative, the people around him put up with a great deal. He was, after all, during the war, irreplaceable. Indeed Britain's war effort was inconceivable without him.

Thus Cadogan during the war had a talk with Anthony Eden complaining that he had to rest during the day because he expected the prime minister to keep him up until 3am.

That such routines had to be accepted as part and parcel of Churchill's wartime leadership was well known. However, their acceptance did not mean that people were not offended and hurt by them.[6]

In 1940, Clementine had written to her husband that his 'rough and sarcastic and overbearing manner was producing either dislike or a slavish mentality'. Clementine's verdict was loving but blunt. 'My darling Winston, I must confess that I have noticed a deterioration in your manner and you are not as kind as you used to be.'[7]

Hurt though many were, Churchill remained well able to persuade and to charm but by 1945, with the end of the war in sight and Labour's growing confidence that they would win the election afterwards, tolerance by his deputy prime minister began to shade into deep dissatisfaction, even disdain.

In January 1945, the Labour Party leader Clement Attlee wrote Churchill a letter. It was the most direct criticism of the nature of Churchill's leadership at that time and it was being made by the only person who could make it. The letter pinpointed a failure of leadership, evident as early as 1940 as testified in his wife's letter to him. Few now doubted that without his leadership Britain could not have survived the war. But the burden of those years had rendered Churchill more fractious and less resourceful. Thus Attlee, who by then knew that the odds were that he would replace Churchill at Number 10, wrote this damning indictment of how Churchill ran the cabinet. Over six pages of systematic criticism Attlee set out why he had 'for some time had it in mind to write to you on the method or rather lack of method of dealing with matters requiring Cabinet decisions'.[8] Its tenor is well illustrated by this excerpt:

> Often half an hour and more is wasted in explaining what could have been grasped by two or three minutes reading of the document. Not infrequently a phrase catches your eye which gives rise to a disquisition on an interesting point only slightly connected with the subject matter. The result is long delays and unnecessarily long Cabinet imposed on Ministers who have already done a full day's work and who will have more to deal with before they get to bed.[9]

Cadogan's irritation had morphed into Attlee's condemnation.

However, as Allen Packwood, curator of the Churchill Archives at Cambridge University, has expressed it to me, Churchill's taut reply 'is not the whole story'. In fact, Jack Colville, Churchill's private secretary and confidant, was present when Churchill received Attlee's letter and described the incident in a document that survives in his papers. According to Colville, Churchill was furious at receiving Attlee's letter. Initially he wanted to make a full reply – a point by point rebuttal – and such a draft survives in his papers. But first Brendan Bracken (Churchill's close friend), then Lord Beaverbrook (his close ally and frequent benefactor) and then Clementine (his ever closest ally but often most insightful critic) all told him that Attlee was right.

On the record, Churchill's reply to Attlee's missive is a characteristically brief, caustic and wounding riposte: 'I have to thank you for your private and personal letter – you may be sure I shall always endeavour to profit by your counsels.'[10] Churchill's feelings were hurt. After replying to Attlee he then told Colville, 'I am deserted by my friends and even by my wife.'

In 1945, as Churchill surveyed the scene, he must have felt not only deserted by his friends and his wife but also deserted by so many of the great certainties that had sustained him in the past. Where was the power of France? Certainly not restored. Where was the wartime Allied coalition? It lay in ruins with Stalin at the gates of the West. Where was the Empire? He knew India would go, and without India what real imperial status would remain for Britain?

On what was Britain's power and influence to be based?

Her economy was nearly bankrupt, her armed forces quite unable to match those of the Soviet and American superpowers. Above all could Britain's friendship with the USA – the Anglo-Saxon partnership so close to his heart – be able to counter Roosevelt's naivety with Stalin? Roosevelt's distrust of the British Empire had deeply shocked Churchill but at least he had known

Roosevelt and won his support in the early desperate stages of the war. Now he was dead and the new man, Truman, had not impressed him at Potsdam.

What chance did he – a defeated prime minister – have to create a new certainty? How could he bring forth a new world order sustainable and strong? Could he once again rally the cause of freedom?

The challenge now before him was to persuade voters on both sides of the Atlantic that defending freedom had not been completed with the defeat of the Axis powers. A farther task awaited the free world, namely containing a tyranny as menacing as Nazism had been before the Second World War. Anthony Montague Browne, who grew close to Churchill after the war, recounts how Churchill dealt with someone who suggested that communist Russia was the antithesis of Nazi Germany. Churchill's argument was this: 'If you were blindfolded and placed on the ice at the South Pole you wouldn't know the difference from the North Pole, which is indeed its antithesis.' His task was to re-orientate the democracies to the reality of a new geography.[11]

In his history of his ancestor, the Duke of Marlborough, Churchill had written of Marlborough's death: 'Noble spirits yield themselves willingly to the successively falling shades which carry them to a better world, or to oblivion.'[12]

Fortunately, by January 1946, as he prepared for America, his purpose was the opposite of oblivion.

6

Outward Bound

On 8 January 1946, the day before he boarded the *Queen Elizabeth* for New York, Winston Churchill made the shorter journey up the Mall to Buckingham Palace. There George VI conferred on him the Order of Merit. As Churchill explained to friends, 'The Order of Merit comes from the King alone and is not given on the advice of Ministers. This renders it more attractive to me.'[1] Months earlier, when Churchill first heard that the king wished to bestow this most prestigious and personal honour upon him, he rejected the idea with trademark self-pity. Why should he receive the OM from the king when he had just received the 'Order of the Boot' from the British people?[2]

But in the New Year, with the prospect of the journey before him, Churchill was already feeling more buoyant. As one who had always lived beyond his means, the costs of being had become crippling with the loss of office. Gone was the support of No. 10 with its endless supply of 'the very best' even during the war. Gone too was the luxury of Chequers, the country residence of the prime minister. On hearing, therefore, just before his departure to the USA that Viscount Camrose was proposing to make Churchill's home at Chartwell 'a national possession' run by the National Trust where Churchill would be able to live until he died, paying an annual rental of only £350, gave him profound relief. It was in

Churchill's view 'a princely plan', and now there was the imminent prospect of the voyage itself.

The 'star-spangled' waves beckoned and as he was to demonstrate, on arrival in New York on 14 January, his sap was rising. His
press conference on landing would be a triumph and certainly
disquieting to Anthony Eden, so desperately waiting in London,
wanting to inherit the crown.

The 81,000 ton *Queen Elizabeth*, freshly sporting funnels
repainted in Cunard red and black, was overall, however, still
decked in her wartime camouflage colours, and was waiting at
the Southampton dockside for the 11am arrival of Churchill's
party – his wife Clementine, his secretary Miss Jo Sturdee, whose
letters to her parents provide much colour to this narrative, a
valet, Mrs Churchill's maid and a police officer. At 2pm the ship
sailed out of Southampton Water under the captaincy of James
Biset. Although still configured to transport troops, Cunard had
established on board the *Queen Elizabeth* a private suite on the
sun deck for the Churchills and reserved a section of the deck for
their sole use.

Churchill spent much time on board on the bridge. It was his
favourite vantage point. On the day before their arrival in New
York he was invited by Commodore Biset to address the crew and
the 12,314 Canadian troops crammed on board returning home.
He ended his remarks by sharing his perspective from the bridge.

Yesterday I was on the bridge, watching the mountainous waves
and this ship, which is no pup, cutting through them and mock-
ing their anger. I asked myself, why is it that that the ship beats
the waves, when they are so many and the ship is one? The reason is that the ship has a purpose and the waves have none. They
just flop around.[3]

The troops on board would remind Winston Churchill vividly of part of his purpose in making the voyage. Cunard's records show that starting on 24 August 1945, with 14,996 US troops returning to New York, the *Queen Elizabeth* was shuttling tens of thousands back home – nearly 15,000 on 14 September alone. America's presence in Western Europe was flooding west while the Red Army stayed put.

On this voyage as on all his others on the two *Queen Elizabeth*s he was revered and coveted. For Cunard there could be no more important passenger. Churchill would have had no cause to repeat the impatient ditty with which he always confronted his doctor, Lord Moran.

> When you need a whisky:
> 'Put your fingers on the bell
> And make it ring like bloody hell!'[4]

The service would have been impeccable but the maps had gone, as had the map room which came as part and parcel with his premiership. He was – to the world at least and as yet – not at the centre of things.

In mid-Atlantic this must have been the tension that gnawed at him – that he had been marginalised by history. He had said to Moran days before the departure: 'There are lots of flies buzzing round this old decaying carcass. I want something to keep them away. I want sun, solitude, serenity, and something to eat and something to drink.' But Moran noted something else. He wrote, 'What he really wants is something quite different. Looking up at me, he said "I think I can be of some use over there. They will take things from me."'[5]

For Churchill this was a voyage of hope. He knew well that he was 'a small lion walking between a huge Russian bear and a great

American elephant'.[6] He also knew that the new president, with whom in a few weeks he would travel to Fulton, believed the US Congress would never sanction US troops remaining in Europe for more than two years. The Cunarders would continue to run from East to West carrying them home. But he also felt in his heart the imperative to match the challenge of the time. From Berlin he had written to his daughter, Sarah: 'Tonight the sun goes down on more suffering than ever before in the World.'[7] But he had always believed in the strength and energy of that sunrise to the West. That was his distinction.

The 'mountainous waves' delayed the arrival in Manhattan by five hours and they docked at 8.30pm on 14 January. It was fine and cold, and their welcome revealed how right his instincts had been – that in the USA they would sit up and take notice. There were hundreds of police and a vast crowd of reporters. Churchill was indeed back at the centre of things. Smoking a large cigar he agreed to an impromptu press conference as soon as he had descended from the gangway. Crammed into a waiting room ablaze with flash bulbs bursting, and noisy with dozens of shouted questions, he went straight to his official remit – a $4 billion loan the United Kingdom was seeking from the United States. 'Some countries were overrun,' he said. 'We were fighting and using up our credit. We borrowed all we could.' But Britain only wanted to be helped 'back on our feet again'. He beamed at his audience, wiping his eyes moist with the impact of the flashlights. This was the consummate political showman coming back on form. Walter Locke, an American journalist, wrote a sketch of him 'round faced, round headed, benevolent, almost jolly . . . a look of genial impishness . . . humour flashes in his face and sparkles in his tongue. He sits slumped . . . this atomic bomb of an Englishman.'[8]

Locke was right to detect the power behind the bonhomie. Asked about his leadership of the Conservative Party his reply was sharp and will have brought little comfort to Anthony Eden reading it in London the next day. 'I have no intention whatever of ceasing to lead the Conservative Party.' As to becoming the first Secretary-General of the United Nations (a proposal being mooted at the time), 'That is the first I've heard of it'.[9] The implication was that it would be the last.

Have a Holiday, Get a Loan

The period between Churchill's disembarkation on 14 January and the delivery of his speech at Fulton on 5 March can be seen as an interlude before the main event. Certainly what he would say at Fulton increasingly dominated his thinking as the weeks went past. Fulton became the drumbeat and, by his return to Washington in the days immediately before boarding the train with Truman, his mind was marching at its pace. Momentum and tension were palpable.

However, Churchill did have other preoccupations. The Attlee government had made it clear that a priority was to try and persuade the Americans to loan substantial funds to the UK. Certainly he was in the United States to enjoy himself in ways he found rejuvenating – receiving the generous hospitality of his Miami host, Colonel Clarke, soaking up the sun to the extent his pale complexion would allow, swimming, painting, drinking, smoking and talking.

But all this could not disguise the imperative of gaining the loan – his unofficial remit. He had to explain to the US authorities Britain's desperate and deserving requirement for, if possible, an interest-free loan to mitigate its huge debts now that Lend-Lease had abruptly and brutally ended. Secretary of State James Byrnes, a tough and sometimes hostile partner for Britain, would travel down to meet Churchill in Miami as would his friend and banker Bernard Baruch. Byrnes would describe the visit as 'purely social'. In Churchill's mind he had summoned both men on the king's business.

The difficulty Churchill encountered on this issue would profoundly influence his later behaviour in 1946. He understood in order to gain American financial generosity for Britain and indeed for Europe the British and the Europeans would have to do more for themselves. His experience in the USA at the beginning of the year shaped his thinking for the speech he would deliver six months later in Zurich.

In the middle of the Florida interlude, Churchill's party crossed over to Cuba.

For Churchill this whole pre-Fulton episode followed the tracks of the past. He had first come to America in 1895 determined to see military action in Cuba where the Spanish were seeking to suppress rebellion, a task Churchill thought they would fail to achieve as certainly as decades later Batista would fall before Castro. Churchill was drawn almost as a moth to a candle by conflict and his good luck in escaping bullets 'that whizzed past his head like demented insects'[1] on several occasions confirmed his life-long imperviousness to physical danger.

Back in 1895 he had travelled to Cuba by the same route. He had crossed to New York by Cunard sailing in their steamship *Etruria*. He had stayed briefly in New York, which delighted him as did the Americans. They were 'great, crude, strong young people' and 'boisterous'.[2] He headed down to Florida by train – the sybarite in him rejoicing in the sun – and then to Cuba, where he not only saw action, escaped death and received his first decoration – from the Spanish – but also discovered Havana cigars which he was to savour for a lifetime and turn into one of the most successful political brands of all time.

Thus Churchill, for whom the past always informed the present and who was also well able to extract pleasure from the moment, built back up his energy and *joie de vivre*.

This was evident from the moment he arrived in Florida. On his arrival in Miami he was immediately immersed in a press conference held on the lawn of Colonel Clarke's home where forty journalists and photographers gathered 'in the shade of coconut palms and luxuriant tropical foliage'. Churchill remarked that it was 'warmer than the Riviera' and had to take off his grey felt hat to mop his brow.[3] He joked about his painting – no, he wouldn't be concentrating on Miami Beach's 'bathing beauties'. 'I am not much good at figures,'[4] he said.

However, he was very clear about the figures involved in the loan Britain needed. 'We have got to face the extraordinary situation of buying food and goods against very heavy odds in our trade balance. We are buying time – time to get on our feet again.'[5] And Britain had the right to ask America for the loan. 'We have suffered more financially than any other country.' Pointedly given America's late entry into the war, he said, 'Other countries were not fighting and using up their credit.' His conclusion was blunt: 'That is why we seek the loan. We went all out and remained the only great unbroken nation from start to finish.'

It was the same argument he would use a few weeks later during James Byrnes' and Baruch's visit to Miami, knowing full well that Byrnes was on record saying that the USA should not extend credits abroad before there had been a full accounting and listing of American assets at home. The Senate would prove difficult.

That opinion on the Hill was so divided on the loan was in part Churchill's fault. Earlier, in the House of Commons, neither Labour nor Tory were satisfied with what had been negotiated. The US negotiations had proved very tough and Britain's brilliant economist

John Maynard Keynes had failed to move them. As Keynes wasp-ishly observed, America tried to 'pick out the eyes of the British Empire'.[6] Truman had cut off Lend-Lease with brutal brusqueness. It seemed that for any new arrangement, Britain would have to pay through the nose. The issue was not the rate of interest, although many Parliamentarians, including Churchill himself, believed that the loan should be interest free – an acknowledgement of what the free world owed Britain for its courage in 1940. The affront most resented by the Tories was the demand that imperial trading arrange-ments be abolished and replaced with a free-trading system that would favour the USA. In particular, the rump Tory Party left in the House of Commons after the party's rout in the 1945 general election feared the impact on British agriculture of American imports. Most of them represented farming constituencies.

Thus it was that, when the government under Attlee brought a bill to the House accepting US terms for the loan, Churchill was constrained and lost control of half his party. The government expected the Tories to back the bill however reluctantly as the best that could be negotiated and far better than insolvency.

Churchill's speech was ambiguous. He was clearly on a cross. He complained about the terms but could not and would not reject the American offer. Bob Boothby and others were contemp-tuous. This was an overt US attack on the British Empire and here was the man, pledged to defend it, now giving it away.

In the end the Tories abstained officially, Churchill sitting out the vote in impotence while half his MPs defied even this half-hearted whip and voted against the bill. Churchill was close to losing the leadership of his party, confirming his distaste for his role as Leader of the Opposition.

In the USA, by contrast, Churchill's abstention on the loan was interpreted as a rejection of the American offer. For many, like

Churchill's friend Baruch, it seemed that as Churchill was against the loan, they did not need to be for it. Opinion in Congress was close and bad tempered. Thus for the loan to pass on the Hill, Churchill needed to clarify his position. His genius was not simply to explain his embarrassment in Westminster, but to use the message that he was preparing for Fulton to pressure the Americans on the loan. The implication of his Iron Curtain speech would be clear: to stop Stalin, Britain had to be supported.

The fact was that Churchill expected US generosity and believed Britain deserved it. The truth was that Churchill had accommodated himself to being disappointed by the Americans. The analogy is used of the lover determined not to be dismayed. Certainly he wooed Roosevelt, Truman's predecessor, with pleas, entreaties and flattery that a medieval troubadour would have envied. And the course of true love became harder as the disparity between British and US power grew greater.

When Churchill met Roosevelt on the USS *Augusta*, in Placentia Bay Newfoundland on 9 August 1941, he was to challenge the president bluntly and emotionally over dinner about his opposition to the British Empire. Roosevelt's hostility towards and occasional derision of Churchill's imperialism is well documented by Roosevelt's son. But in that year the USA had no troops engaged in Europe. Roosevelt's hostility to the British Empire did not give him any moral high ground – that belonged to Churchill because Britain was fighting Hitler alone. The military deployment was Churchill's, but he knew the reality of British weakness. He had the right and the nerve to display his anger at Roosevelt's presumption but, ultimately, his task was to win America's support both militarily and monetarily.

But by D-Day, and every week thereafter, the disparity of power yawned wider. Churchill's relations with Roosevelt deteriorated.

The prime minister felt himself snubbed and British interests endangered by Roosevelt's wooing of Stalin. The USA had decided to give clear preference to the USSR within the Grand Alliance and, at a personal level, Churchill found it very difficult to take.

We cannot know how great a factor this became in the prime minister's hesitancy about attending Roosevelt's funeral in April 1945. His eventual decision not to attend surprised everyone on both sides of the Atlantic – particularly the new President Truman.

Many years later – on 15 October 1951 – Churchill was travelling by train from an election meeting he had addressed in Huddersfield. He was accompanied by Lady Violet Bonham Carter, Lord Layton and his own doctor, Lord Moran. Dinner was served and, emboldened by Churchill's mood, Lord Layton asked him provocatively (according to Moran's diaries):

> 'Tell us, Winston, what was your biggest mistake . . . in the war?'[7]
>
> Churchill did not hesitate.
>
> 'I've no doubt at all. Not going to meet Truman after Roosevelt's death. During the next three months, tremendous decisions were made and I had a feeling that they were being made by a man I did not know. It wasn't my fault. I wanted to cross the Atlantic. But Anthony [Eden] put me off. He telegraphed from Washington that they did not want me.'[8]

Certainly Churchill discarded the opportunity to meet him and talk in depth after the funeral. That he missed this chance then will have contributed to the alacrity with which he accepted the invitation to Fulton.

A Synthesis of Agendas

For Churchill the motivation at the core of his wooing of America and its president was not a desire to be at the centre of events nor to recapture celebrity status – what drove him was not psychology but ideology. He saw Soviet power as a mortal threat. He believed an understanding with the Soviets was obtainable but only if the West displayed determination and force. At Yalta he had accepted Stalin's promises but in his heart had not believed them. Roosevelt had. The time had come to compel Stalin to show his cards.

The paragraphs that follow delineate the deep roots of Churchill's antagonism, tempered as it was by his recognition of what Russian courage and sacrifice had achieved in the war.

As we have seen, in proposing a toast in Moscow in October 1944, Churchill acknowledged this debt with complete sincerity. He knew well what tearing the 'guts out of the filthy Nazis'[1] had involved. From the launch of Barbarossa by Hitler on 22 June 1941 and D-Day on 6 June 1944, 93 per cent of German military casualties were inflicted by Soviet forces – 4.2 million German troops missing, wounded or killed. The cost to Russia was around 20 million casualties, civilian and military.

Churchill's admiration, even veneration, of Russian sacrifice during the war did not mask his deep repugnance of Bolshevism. He had ordered Britain's Arctic convoys to supply arms to Russia at an awful cost in casualties. He was clear that the menace of Hitler required that he do everything possible to sustain Russia, but this did not diminish his acute awareness of the threat of Bolshevism and the brutality of the Soviet regime. Roosevelt was less sure.

It is because of this that his Fulton speech was to have such 'bottom'. As Britain's Minister of War in 1919 he had backed military intervention in the Russian Civil War. In 1920 he described the Bolsheviks as having driven 'man from the civilization of the 20th century into a condition of barbarism'.[2] By 1942 he was already warning that 'it would be a measureless disaster if Russian barbarism overlaid the culture and independence of the ancient States of Europe'.[3] And after this had happened he told the House of Commons in a debate in 1949 that 'the strangling of Bolshevism at its birth would have been an untold blessing to the human race'.[4]

Thus Churchill's loathing of Bolshevism was curtailed by the exigencies of the Second World War but it was not repudiated by him either privately or, on occasion, publicly. In the run-up to Fulton, Churchill felt the moment had come to beat 'the crocodile' over the head, and what convinced him of this were the events that concluded the war. They revealed Stalin's intentions all too clearly. For Churchill, Stalin's behaviour at Yalta and Potsdam was particularly galling as he felt he had been duped by Stalin's promises to establish a form of democracy in the countries conquered by the Red Army.

For Churchill, two events were seminal. The first occurred in August 1944 when Stalin halted the Red Army, then sixty miles from Warsaw. There they waited while the SS annihilated the Warsaw uprising killing 250,000 civilians and condemning half a million to concentration camps. Stalin refused to allow the Western

Allies to fly in supplies to help Poland's Home Army from bases in the Ukraine and his refusal shattered America's ambassador in Moscow, Averell Harriman, who had pleaded for it.

Churchill was also outraged by Stalin's ruthlessness, though not surprised. After all, Stalin had stated clearly that 'This war is not as in the past: whoever occupies a territory also imposes on it his own social system – as far as his army can reach.'[5] Days before Fulton, Stalin publicly amplified this message. Capitalism and communism could never co-exist. His message was that war was the inevitable result of capitalism.

It is at this point that Churchill's journey to America and to Fulton crosses the trajectory of another powerful warning of Soviet intent also spurred by the recent events. This is what became known as the 'long telegram' written by George Kennan, the number 2 at the American embassy in Moscow. As I have mentioned before, it arrived in Washington two weeks before Fulton and was unknown to the public. It was secret, unreported in the press and unknown to the public. In the administration it caused a sensation. There is no conclusive evidence that the text was read by either Truman or Churchill, but the former would have been warned of its contents by Secretary of State Byrnes and the latter almost certainly by Kennan's boss, Averell Harriman. Kennan had arrived in Moscow in July 1944 to serve under Harriman who authorised him to write this famous report of Soviet intentions – the 'long telegram'. In Washington, they didn't take much notice of Kennan's warnings but, like Churchill, he had a laser-like ability to focus on events and, spurred by these, he took his opportunity in February 1946.

Kennan wrote his telegram in bed. He was down with flu. In Washington the Treasury, shocked by Russia's refusal to co-operate in setting up the International Monetary Fund and World Bank,

(350)

WESTMINSTER COLLEGE

CHARTERED IN 1853

FULTON, MISSOURI

October 3, 1945

The Honorable Winston Churchill, M. P.
London
England

W.S.C.

My dear Mr. Churchill:

In 1936 an English-born woman, Mrs. John Findley Green, estab-lished at Westminster College a memorial lectureship to be known as the John Findley Green Foundation. The lectureship was established to bring to the college campus each year a man of international reputation who would discuss economic, social, or political problems of international concern in a series of three or four lectures. After the lectures are delivered, the lecturer leaves the manuscript with the college in order that they may be published in book form.

This letter is to invite you to deliver the Green Lectures in the winter of 1945-1946, or in the spring of 1946. We should be glad to arrange the date or dates to suit your convenience.

The arrangement for the scheduling of the lectures may be made to suit your convenience. It had been our thought to have one lecture at the college one evening and to have another lecture delivered in St. Louis, Missouri (U.S.A.) on the evening of the following day. The college is located one hundred miles from this metropolitan center and we should like to arrange for your appearance under the auspices of the Green Found-ation before the great audience which would assemble in St. Louis to hear you. We know that any discussions coming from you and delivered from this forum here in the heart of the United States will be of immense and endur-ing significance, and will promote the international understanding requisite to the maintenance of peace. We earnestly hope that you will do us the honor of accepting this invitation.

A suitable honorarium will be provided. In this instance, we shall also be glad to allow you to arrange for the publication of the lectures, or we shall make the arrangement and allow you to share in the royalties.

Enclosed you will find excerpt from the Instrument of Gift, estab-lishing the John Findley Green Foundation Lectureship at Westminster College.

This is a wonderful school in my home state. Hope you can do it. I'll introduce you. Best regards,
Harry Truman

Yours respectfully,

F. L. McCluer
President

FLM:D
enclosure (1)

Letter of invitation from the president of Westminster College in Fulton, Missouri to Sir Winston Churchill, with a personal note from President Truman encouraging him to accept, 3 October 1945.

Sir Winston and Clementine Churchill disembarking from the RMS *Queen Elizabeth* in New York for a trip combining business and pleasure, 14 January 1946.

Sir Winston Churchill with Edward Wood, Lord Halifax, at the airport in Washington D.C. after a visit to President Truman as Churchill heads to Florida, 16 February 1946.

Sir Winston Churchill relaxing on the palm-fringed shores of De Lido Island in Biscayne Bay at Miami Beach. Churchill painted to relax and stave off depression.

Sir Winston Churchill and President Truman leave for Fulton, Missouri, where Churchill gave the Sinews of Peace speech, also known as the Iron Curtain speech, 1 March 1946.

personal contact with the President.

2.   The above strikes me as a very important act of state and
one calculated to make Russia understand that she must come to
reasonable terms of discussion with the Western Democracies.   From our
point of view, I am sure that the arrival and stay of such a powerful
American Fleet in the Straits must be entirely beneficial, both as
reassuring Turkey and Greece and as placing a demurrer on what Bevin
called cutting our life-line through the Mediterranean by the
establishment of a Russian naval base at Tripoli.

3.   I did not consult the President on the exact text of my
speech at Fulton before I finished it, but he read a mimiographed
reproduction which was made on the train in its final form, several
hours before I delivered it.   He told me he thought it was admirable
and would do nothing but good, though it would make a stir.   He
seemed equally pleased during and after.   I also showed it to
Mr. Byrnes the night before leaving Washington, making it clear that
this was quite private and informal.   He was excited about it and
did not suggest any alterations.   Admiral Leahy, to whom I showed it
first of all, was enthusiastic.   Naturally I take complete and sole
personal responsibility for what I said, for I altered nothing as the
result of my contacts with these high American authorities.   I think

Proof from the papers of Sir Winston Churchill that President Truman read the
speech on the train prior to Churchill speaking at Fulton.

President Truman, Sir Winston Churchill and Dr. Franc McCluer, the president of Westminster College, walking to Westminster College where Churchill gave the Sinews of Peace speech, 5 March 1946.

Peep under the Iron Curtain by Leslie Illingworth, 6 March 1946.

Sir Winston Churchill and General Dwight D. Eisenhower en route to Richmond, Virginia, 8 March 1946.

Sir Winston Churchill, General Dwight D. Eisenhower and their wives at Colonial Williamsburg, 8 March 1946.

Prime Minister Clement Attlee and Sir Winston Churchill at the London Victory
Celebrations, 8 June 1946.

During the Potsdam Conference, Sir Winston Churchill and Sir Anthony Eden tour the ruins of a pulverised Berlin, 16 July 1945.

Sir Winston and Clementine Churchill flying to Switzerland with their daughter Mary.

Sir Winston Churchill giving his United States of Europe speech in the Münsterhof in Zurich, Switzerland, 19 September 1946.

Sir Winston Churchill giving his U for unity sign at the Münsterhof in Zurich, Switzerland, 19 September 1946

Sir Winston Churchill and Clementine being toasted following his speech in Zurich, 19 September 1946.

I am ~~going~~ now going to say something that will astonish you.
The first step in the re-creation of the European family must be
a partnership between France and Germany.   There can be no
revival of Europe without a spiritually great France and a
spiritually great Germany.   The structure of the United States
of Europe, if well and truly built, ~~would~~ will be such as to make the
material strength of a single state less important.   Small
nations ~~would~~ will count as much as large ones and ~~shine~~ gain their honour by their
contribution to the common cause.   The ancient states and
principalities of Germany, freely joined together for mutual
convenience in a federal system, might each take their independent place
among the United States of Europe.   I shall not try to make
a detailed programme ~~blue prints~~ for hundreds of millions of people who want to be
happy and free, prosperous and safe, who wish to enjoy the four
freedoms of which the great President Roosevelt spoke, and live
in accordance with the principles embodied in the Atlantic
Charter.   If this is ~~there~~ their wish, ~~surely machinery can~~ they have only to say so, & certainly be
~~devised,~~ and means can certainly be found, to carry it into that wish
~~effect~~ full fruition.
all persons
at .

Example of Sir Winston Churchill's attention to detail in his annotated speech in
Zurich. Note the key addition of the word 'now' within 'I am now going to say
something that will astonish you' prior to proposing a United States of Europe.

-6-

of man?   If it can, the wrongs and injuries which have been

inflicted will have been washed away on all sides by the agony

which has been endured.   Is there any need for further floods

of misery?   Is the only lesson of history that mankind is

unteachable?   Let there be justice, mercy and

freedom.   The peoples have only to will it, and all will achieve their

hearts' desire.

© Churchill Archives Centre, Churchill College, The Papers of Sir Winston Churchill

Lord Watson being awarded the Churchill Medal by Lady Soames, Winston Churchill's daughter, in 2005 in recognition of his extraordinary achievement in the promotion of English as an international language.

pleaded with the State Department for an explanation. They in turn asked their embassy in Moscow to provide one and, as we have seen, Harriman was happy for Kennan to reply. As Kennan confided in his memoirs, 'They [the State Department] had asked for it. Now by God they would have it!'[6] In 5,000 words he spelled out Soviet realities as he saw them. His message was simple, however: it was imperative now to smite the crocodile.

The Yalta Protocol was signed by Stalin and accepted by Roosevelt and Churchill. This stated that the liberated peoples of Eastern Europe should be allowed to create democratic institutions of their own choice. In Kennan's view this pledge was not worth the paper it was written upon.[7] Roosevelt may have believed it, Churchill may have wished to, but events revealed a different and chilling reality.

In the 'long telegram', Kennan had confirmed what was happening. Now it was for Churchill to give the clarion call. He now returned to Washington to finalise the speech he hoped would do the job of alerting the Americans and the world to what needed to be done. Containment would become imperative and the unique Anglo-American alliance the means of achieving it.

Crucially his political imagination was binding together a synthesis of agendas. One was that the Anglo-American alliance was essential if Stalin was to be stopped and his bridgehead strategy of further European expansion frustrated. The USA had to be persuaded to defend Europe.

For that, America's unique ally in Europe – the United Kingdom – had to survive economically. This meant the administration had to deliver on the loan Britain desperately needed following the cessation of Lend-Lease. And thus we come to the second part of Churchill's agenda. It wasn't only saving Britain economically. Europe had to be saved and more importantly it

had to be seen by the Americans to be worth saving. Europe had
to become economically and politically viable. Churchill was clear
that for this to happen Europe would have to unite, profoundly
unlikely though that prospect seemed in 1946.

Churchill's political instinct was pushing him towards a magi-
cian's touch. At Fulton he would call for an Anglo-American
alliance militarily capable of containing Soviet expansionism –
using the unique window of a temporary atomic monopoly. He
would also push his case for the loan to Britain from the USA. But
he would also put down the marker for a second speech – the one
he would give in Zurich later in the year and a speech that would
astonish the world by calling for Franco-German partnership.

PART III

CHURCHILL'S CRUSADE

9

Lord Halifax and the White House

Churchill's travel plans were never simple and always subject to whim. He loved the indulgence of changing his mind. When he arrived in Washington, on 10 February 1946, he was not as free to alter arrangements as on previous visits. He was no longer prime minister and thus was not invited to stay in the White House. During the war he had virtually been given a wing of the presidential mansion. However, the food was dire and he loathed Roosevelt's cocktails – preferring surreptitiously to fortify himself on visits to the lavatory from a flask of Johnnie Walker whisky. But he had been Roosevelt's guest at the epicentre of power. Now he was relegated to the British embassy – so near yet so far. And to make matters worse, his host was not the president but instead Lord Halifax – the man he had sent to Washington in 1940 to get him out of London.

During May 1940 Lord Halifax, in cabinet, was unhappy with Churchill's resolute objection to any form of negotiation with Hitler either directly or through Italian intermediaries. Churchill believed the British people would find any terms repugnant unless they had joined battle to the last. The Labour Party agreed. Halifax, who had so nearly become prime minster on Neville Chamberlain's resignation and who was the preferred choice of the king and many Tory MPs, took a very different view. He favoured seeking the mediation of Mussolini and in talking with the Italian ambassador had even contemplated putting the future of Gibraltar, Malta and Suez on the negotiating table.[1]

Churchill's style infuriated Halifax. 'I have seldom met anybody with stranger gaps of knowledge or whose mind works in greater jerks . . .'[2] After the key war cabinet meeting on 27 May 1940 he condemned Churchill as talking 'the most awful rot'. He threatened to resign and Churchill later would, in effect, accept it and send him to Washington as ambassador. It was not that Halifax proposed treason. He believed he proposed reason – negotiate before risking defeat. Churchill believed there could be no negotiation unless defeated and in these circumstances he and the rest of the cabinet should be prepared to 'choke in their own blood'. Surrender would be left to others and, astonishingly, he had the aged Lloyd George in mind as a British Pétain.

We now know from German Colonel General Franz Halder's war diaries that Adolf Hitler had indeed started to think along similar lines. He suggested during a planning conference for Operation Sea Lion, the German invasion of the United Kingdom, that a British cabinet might be formed consisting of Lloyd George, Chamberlain and Lord Halifax.

None of this had come to pass but on arriving in Washington on 10 February 1946, with Halifax as his host, Churchill may well have sensed that his determination to throw down the gauntlet to another tyrant, Stalin, might evoke the same trepidation in Halifax as when he had defied Hitler. In the event that is precisely what happened.

They all had dinner together on the evening of the 10th, where Jo Sturdee, Churchill's secretary, was present. A letter to her parents not only includes a drawing of the table plan – Lady Halifax on Churchill's left, Lord Halifax at the head – but also her verdict on the occasion. It was, she wrote, 'exhausting, small and very polite talk. Dreary, dreary, dreary!'[3] Churchill was not going to unwind with Halifax beside him.

At 10.00pm, the 'dreary' dinner complete, Churchill left for the White House for a private meeting about the arrangements for Fulton. Media interest was intense but the next day the White House spokesman had little to say. Churchill and Truman had talked in the president's study and it was 'almost wholly'[4] to do with their journey to Fulton. In fact they were to go by train. Press Secretary Charles Ross was insistent that the conversation between the two men had 'not been on any political matter or on the British loan'. However, this very first encounter with Truman at the White House signalled that things were not quite as they seemed.[5]

So, what did the two men talk about that night? The correspondent of *The Times* of London was in little doubt. 'Obviously when a speech is made by the former Prime Minister and present Head of the Opposition in the British Parliament under the virtual sponsorship of the head of the American Government, reasons of policy and courtesy demand that its contents and emphasis should be known to the President in advance.'[6] Undoubtedly this was the case. For the first time therefore we encounter the ambiguity surrounding this 'most important' speech of Churchill's life. Later and often, Truman was to deny any advance knowledge of what Churchill was to say at Fulton. That deception begins with his press secretary's denial on 11 February that anything of any political significance had been discussed in the president's study on 10 February.

Churchill slept in on the morning of the 11th. His meeting with Truman had been demanding. He will have risen with pleasure because the embassy's guests for lunch were General

Eisenhower and his wife. Eisenhower and Churchill got on famously at that time, and they were to meet again after Fulton when both visited Richmond and Williamsburg.

We have no record of what they said to each other at lunch on the 11th but the conversation was more animated than the 'dreary, dreary' dinner with the Halifaxes the night before. As tension was rising with the Soviets the subject might well have been raised by either man. George Kennan's telegram had not yet arrived. It reached Washington on the 22nd after Churchill had returned to Miami, but the disquiet which prompted the State Department to request the views of the US embassy in Moscow would have been common ground between Eisenhower and Churchill. Sturdee has left us the table plan but no record of table talk.

The Churchills departed back to Florida where Churchill would again paint and swim, and start the final formulation of his speech, which he was entitling 'The Sinews of Peace'. It was not a title that would stick – this was to become known as the 'Iron Curtain' speech and as such the first significant salvo of the Cold War.

The Train to Missouri

The Churchills returned to Washington from Miami by train on 1 March. Even this straightforward journey had been complicated by Churchillian whimsy. Sturdee wrote to her parents:

> After the usual umpteen changes of plans about whether to fly or to travel to Washington by train . . . write a nice letter . . . Get me Lord someone or other on the phone. Fetch me a whisky and soda. What *are* you doing? Now don't run away and leave me with nothing to do! Grunt, grunt grumble, grumble, mumble.[1]

Churchill was being his most demanding. The great man could be exasperating but, as Sturdee also confessed to her parents, everyone loved him.[2]

Churchill was buoyed up. Attlee sent encouragement from London. 'I am sure your Fulton speech will do good.'[3] He had also outlined the speech to Secretary of State Byrnes and told Attlee 'he seemed to like it very well'.[4]

All looked fair, the prospects good. And then again logistics complicated matters. Sturdee, on whom Churchill was dependent for the finalisation and presentation of the speech which he was constantly altering, had assumed that she would not be on the train to Missouri. In the flurry of arrangements and rearrangements before the party eventually boarded the president's train on 4 March, Churchill kept on demanding things of her. 'What have you done with my red pen? Tell the Ambassador I want to see him. Haven't you opened the post yet?' She explained to him that she could not answer all his questions because she had to put his speech together 'before you leave'. 'Why?' 'Because I'm not coming.' After all no one had asked her. 'Of course you must come. If you can't come I shall have to fly.' Given the importance Churchill gave to his train journey with Truman this was indeed heavy pressure. She concluded to her parents, 'So we all ran around in circles and . . . in the end . . . I tagged along feeling just like another piece of baggage . . . very self-conscious about the fuss caused by my being added at the last minute – the shy female.'[5]

It was just as well she was included because Churchill continued to make changes to the speech until the very end. He also tried a press release about the Anglo-American alliance, which the president's party did not like. Without Sturdee there might well have not been a finalised, readable text for Churchill next day in the Westminster College gymnasium.

In the event, the speech was completed on board the train and shown to Truman, Byrnes, Admiral Leahy and the others. Churchill and Truman had sat up drinking and playing poker until after 2.30 in the morning but at light 'steaming beside the broad Missouri river'[6] Churchill showed the president the final text. What is more he mimeographed it and gave copies to the president and the others present. As he later reported to Bevin the president 'told me he thought it was admirable and would do nothing but good'. Significantly Truman added 'though it will make a stir!'[7]

Churchill's report of what happened on board the train was telegrammed to Bevin on 7 March after the speech. It remains the most detailed account. No reference is made to Kennan's 'long telegram', which by then had arrived and Admiral Leahy, at least, had read, but the on-board discussion was dominated by Soviet moves on Iran and Turkey and the planned US response. This created an environment in which it would have been odd indeed if Truman, Leahy and Byrnes had not endorsed Churchill's text which they were now able to read in its final form.

The text of Churchill's cable to Bevin is as follows:[8]

1. The President told me, as we started on our journey from Washington to Fulton, Missouri, that the United States is sending the body of the Turkish Ambassador, who died here some days ago, back to Turkey in the American battleship MISSOURI, which is the vessel on which the Japanese surrender was signed and is probably the strongest battleship afloat. He added that the MISSOURI would be accompanied by a strong task force, which would remain in the Marmara for an unspecified period. Admiral Leahy told me that the task force would consist of another battleship of the greatest power, two of the largest and strongest aircraft carriers, several cruisers and about a dozen destroyers, with the necessary ancillary ships. Both mentioned the fact that the MISSOURI class carry over 140 anti-aircraft guns. I asked about the secrecy of this movement and was told that it was known that the body of the late Ambassador was being returned in a warship but that the details of the task force would not become known before March 15. I feel it my duty to report these facts to you though it is quite possible you may have already been informed through other channels. At any rate, please on no account, make use of the information until you have received it from channels, other than my personal contact with the President.

2. The above strikes me as a very important act of state and one
   calculated to make Russia understand that she must come to
   reasonable terms of discussion with the Western Democracies.
   From our point of view, I am sure that the arrival and stay of
   such a powerful American Fleet in the Straits must be entirely
   beneficial, both as reassuring Turkey and Greece and as placing
   a restraint on what Beria called cutting our life-line through
   the Mediterranean by the establishment of a Russian naval
   base at Tripoli.

3. I did not consult the President on the exact text of my speech
   at Fulton before I finished it, but he read the mimeographed
   reproduction, which was made on the train in its final form,
   several hours before I delivered it. He told me he thought
   it was admirable and would do nothing but good, though it
   would make a stir. He seemed equally pleased during and
   after. I also showed it to Mr. Byrnes the night before leaving
   Washington, making it clear that this was quite private and
   informal. He was excited about it and did not suggest any
   alterations. Admiral Leahy, to whom I showed it first of all,
   was enthusiastic. Naturally I take complete and sole personal
   responsibility for what I said, for I altered nothing as the result
   of my contacts with these high American authorities. I think
   you ought to know exactly what the position is and hope you
   will understand the very strong and precise terms in which I
   disclaim any official mission or status of any kind and that I
   spoke only for myself. If necessary these words of mine could
   be quoted.

4. Having spent nearly three days in most intimate, friendly contact with the President and his immediate circle, and also having had a long talk with Mr. Byrnes, I have no doubt that the
   Executive forces here are deeply disturbed at the way they are

being treated by Russia and that they do not intend to put up with treaty breaches in Persia or encroachments in Manchuria and Korea, or pressure for the Russian expansion at the exposure of Turkey or in the Mediterranean. I am convinced that some show of strength and resisting power is necessary to a good settlement with Russia. I predict that this will be the prevailing opinion in the United States in the near future.

The high drama of the USS *Missouri*'s steaming to the Sea of Marmara with the corpse of the Turkish ambassador on board, and then staying there with all its mighty firepower available as a warning to the Soviets, would have vastly appealed to Churchill. So too would the tokenism of deploying the battleship on which only the year before imperial Japan had unconditionally surrendered.

Sensing and hoping for the furore his Fulton speech would generate, Churchill was careful to emphasise that he took 'complete responsibility' for the speech and disclaimed 'any official mission or status'. But he would speak with the president beside him, he would speak under 'his aegis' and he had Attlee's support in his pocket. He would fly the kite but with their full connivance. The scene was finally set for Fulton.

II

'The most important speech of my life'

There was no railroad to Fulton itself. They all had to disembark at Jefferson City – a twenty-mile drive away. It was 10.30 in the morning and a warm spring day. A convoy of cars awaited them, first a large open presidential car in which Churchill and Truman would travel as soon as they reached Fulton. It seemed that up to 40,000 people were cramming the streets waiting to glimpse and welcome them. There were two closed cars. In one Churchill and Truman would ride until the moment to switch to the open vehicle. The other was for Sturdee, still incredulous that she was there, Colonel Clarke and Frank Sawyers.

The cars started on their way and the ever observant Sturdee noted that there were crowds all along the route 'all very well dressed, smiling, well looking but very orderly'.[1] Fulton was described to Winston as the 'heart of America'. Certainly it was at the heart of the Midwest – Truman country. As Churchill was to emphasise a few hours later in his speech, this was a country 'at the pinnacle of world power'. The USA has prospered from the war. The evident contentment and prosperity of the Midwest folk lining the roads reflected the strength of America and it was to their strength and the 'awe-inspiring accountability to the future' that this conferred that Churchill was about to appeal. He must have felt he had his finger on the pulse of the great nation he saw as his second home.

At this moment – as so often with Churchill – logistics intervened. Suddenly the car in which Sturdee was travelling 'started smoking out of everywhere and gave out on us'.[2] The convoy halted. They had to transfer to the still empty and open presidential car, and she was soon 'bowling along the roads at 70 mph – hair flying'. It was, she wrote to her parents, 'the nearest I will ever get to fame'. And it didn't last. Churchill and Truman had to seat themselves for the crowds and both of them did so, looking at Sturdee as if to say 'What do you mean by riding in our car?'[3]

Fulton itself had taken on the appearance of a country fair and a political rally. The *Daily Telegraph*'s reporter assured British readers that in Fulton 'Isolationism is unknown. People speak of Mr. Churchill not as a foreign statesman but as one of their own great heroes.'[4] All the streets were decked with flags. People were sporting 'Churchill–Truman Day' badges, three bands were blaring away, loudspeakers had been set up throughout the town and would relay the speeches to 40,000 people and radio would broadcast the event to the world. The town's fourteen policemen had been joined by 500 state troopers. Fulton had never seen anything like it and, although famous political leaders have visited since, no event has matched the impact of Churchill.

Dr McCluer, who had sent the invitation to Churchill, now sat in the open car between him and the president as they drove up to his home. As president of the college he was the host. Members of his board and faculty would join them for a lunch of locally cured ham – the gastronomic pride of Fulton's farmers.

Fulton was a dry county and Westminster a Presbyterian institution. What they all wanted and doubtless needed was a drink. Sturdee tells the tale:

Back everyone troops to the President of the College's house gasping for a drink. No drink as it is a Presbyterian house.

Fortunately though Dr. Harris who was looking after Mrs. Churchill in Florida and who had been requested by the Churchills to come along . . . had brought along a little 'just in case of anything'. So one by one we were tapped on the shoulder and informed that Dr. Harris thought we needed medical attention and would we step in there – a WC. <u>Ah heaven</u> – and each came staggering out feeling the world was a friendlier place after all.[5]

Meanwhile the meal was enjoyed by the sixty people crowded into the college president's house and promptly, at 3pm, resplendent in their *honoris causa* regalia, Truman and Churchill entered the college gymnasium next door.

It was packed to the ceiling with tiers of seats and 2,800 guests. One hundred press and radio reporters and cameramen added to the scene in an atmosphere that crackled with excitement. The college chapel and three churches were used as overflow halls. All was ready for a speech expected by the press to be 'one of his greatest orations'.[6]

The Governor of Missouri, Mr Donnelly, began proceedings by welcoming Churchill to the 'heart of America'. Then Truman made good on his promise to introduce Churchill: 'One of the greatest pleasures and privileges I have had since I have been President.'[7] Finally it was Churchill's turn. The speech, which had first been billed as 'World Affairs' and then 'World Peace' and eventually 'The Sinews of Peace', boomed across the hall. It was relayed to the thousands outside by loudspeaker and to the millions around the United States and the world by radio including Andrei Gromyko, the Soviet foreign minister, then visiting Canada, who was later to condemn it as 'a bad speech'.[8]

However, in the Fulton gymnasium it seemed to go down exceptionally well. There were so many bursts of applause that

Churchill had to pause intermittently, theatrically examining his gold pocket watch – they were stealing his minutes, after all.

It took forty-five minutes to deliver and Churchill clearly enjoyed every second. It was a speech of destiny. He was at the very centre of the world's attention. Beside him the president of the USA was joining, sometimes leading, the applause. He knew he had Attlee's support. He wanted to create more than a stir. He wanted to change the landscape. He was building his legacy.

The speech itself was complex, multi-faceted and conspicuously Victorian in some of its language and sentiment. It ticked the boxes it had to tick. There is his disclaimer that he does not speak for any government, especially his own or that of the United States. It was Truman's wish that he give his 'true and faithful counsel in these anxious and baffling times'.[9] Churchill will do so 'because any private ambitions I [Churchill] may have cherished in my younger days have been satisfied beyond my wildest dreams'.[10] He had fulfilled his ambitions and thus could bring objectivity to what he had to say. Of course, as became evident, the speech itself was about to reignite his further ambition to return to Number 10.

Churchill was well aware of the support he needed to give to the priorities of Roosevelt, thus his support for the new United Nations Organisation. Accordingly, he carefully avoided any criticism of Roosevelt, and his painfully obvious preference in his final months for Stalin's advice rather than that of the prime minister.

When, before the war, he had sought to raise the alarm that tyranny and war threatened the world he had 'cried aloud to my own fellow countrymen and to the world but no one paid any attention'. Now it had to be different.

Before we go to the full text of the Fulton speech, there is one other aspect to underline. It is the Victorian imagery and the perception of reality as Churchill saw it. The world was stalked by 'two giant marauders – war and tyranny'.[11] War could 'dissolve the frame of civilised society . . . confronting humble folk with difficulties with which they could not cope. For them all is distorted, all is broken, even ground to pulp.'[12] In Churchill's mind's eye did he see not only the battlefields in Russia and in Germany but the pulverised cities of Germany and Japan? Churchill had wept upon viewing the film footage of the destruction of Dresden. 'Has it come to this?' he had asked, to the dismay of Air Marshal Harris, head of Bomber Command. Later he circulated a memorandum stating, 'It seems to me that the moment has come when the question of bombing of German cities simply for the sake of increasing the terror, though under other pretexts, should be reviewed'.

As to tyranny, Churchill, in a remarkable passage, describes what he seeks to protect: 'the myriad cottage or apartment homes' where liberty should be protected 'where the title deeds of freedom should lie' – Magna Carta, the Bill of Rights, the Habeas Corpus, trial by jury, the English common law and 'their most famous expression in the American Declaration of Independence'. Clearly he does not intend this to be taken literally but for him these are the priceless assets the Anglo-American inheritance needed now more than ever. It is a coincidence but a compelling one that the *Queen Elizabeth*, which had brought him to America in January, returned to Southampton carrying a Magna Carta which, during the war, had been in the safe keeping of the US government and now returned to Britain stowed under the bed of Commodore Biset.

Embedded in Churchill's speech, itself a grand canvas of his concerns and beliefs, there is one paragraph that presages the speech he was subsequently to give at Zurich. It also echoes earlier expressions of his anxiety that the Soviet advance to the heart of

Europe could result in Nazi dictatorship being replaced by Russian tyranny. In 1942 he had sent a memo to Anthony Eden arguing that a new form of democratic European union would be needed to counter this threat.

Now, in 1946, months before his call at Zurich for a European partnership, he told his Fulton audience that 'the safety of the world requires a new unity in Europe, from which no nation should be permanently outcast'. What he was referring to was Germany.

The significance of this passage in the Fulton speech was missed by the press, the public and the politicians at the time but the signal was clear: Churchill was embarking on a grand new design. His ambition was nothing less than the construction of the ever-elusive alliance between Britain and the USA as well as a reconstructed Western Europe – the only unions that could, and in the event, would, hamper Stalin's own ambition.

Here, then, is the text of Churchill's speech:

Fulton, Missouri, 5 March 1946, by Winston Churchill

I am glad to come to Westminster College this afternoon, and am complimented that you should give me a degree. The name 'Westminster' is somehow familiar to me. I seem to have heard of it before. Indeed, it was at Westminster that I received a very large part of my education in politics, dialectic, rhetoric, and one or two other things. In fact we have both been educated at the same time, or similar, or, at any rate, kindred establishments.

It is also an honour, perhaps almost unique, for a private visitor to be introduced to an academic audience by the President of the United States. Amid his heavy burdens, duties, and responsibilities – unsought but not recoiled from – the President has travelled a thousand miles to dignify and magnify our meeting here today and to give me an opportunity of addressing this kindred nation, as well as my own countrymen across the ocean, and perhaps some other countries too. The President has told you that it is his wish, as I am sure it is yours, that I should have full liberty to give my true and faithful counsel in these anxious and baffling times. I shall certainly avail myself of this freedom, and feel the more right to do so because any private ambitions I may have cherished in my younger days have been satisfied beyond my wildest dreams. Let me, however, make it clear that I have no official mission or status of any kind, and that I speak only for myself. There is nothing here but what you see.

I can therefore allow my mind, with the experience of a lifetime, to play over the problems which beset us on the morrow of our absolute victory in arms, and to try to make sure with what strength I have that what has been gained with so much sacrifice and suffering shall be preserved for the future glory and society of mankind.

The United States stands at this time at the pinnacle of world power. It is a solemn moment for the American Democracy. For with primacy in power is also joined an awe-inspiring accountability to the future. If you look around, you must feel not only the sense of duty done but also you must feel anxiety lest you fall below the level of achievement. Opportunity is here now, clear and shining for both our countries. To reject it or ignore it or fritter it away will bring upon us all the long reproaches of the after-time. It is necessary that constancy of mind, persistency of purpose and the grand simplicity of decision shall guide and rule the conduct of the English-speaking peoples in peace as they did in war. We must, and I believe we shall, prove ourselves equal to this severe requirement.

When American military men approach some serious situation they are wont to write at the head of their directive the words 'overall strategic concept'. There is a wisdom in this, as it leads to clarity of thought. What then is the overall strategic concept, which we should inscribe today? It is nothing less than the safety and welfare, the freedom and progress, of all the homes and families of all the men and women in all the lands. And here I speak particularly of the myriad cottage or apartment homes where the wage-earner strives amid the accidents and difficulties of life to guard his wife and children from privation and bring the family up in the fear of the Lord, or up on ethical conceptions which often play their potent part.

To give security to these countless homes, they must be shielded from the two giant marauders, war and tyranny. We all know the frightful disturbances in which the ordinary family is plunged when the curse of war swoops down upon the bread-winner and those for whom he works and contrives. The awful ruin of Europe, with all its vanished glories, and large parts of Asia glares us in the eyes. When the designs of wicked men or the aggressive urge of mighty states dissolve over large areas the frame of civilised society, humble folk are confronted with difficulties with which they cannot cope. For them all is distorted, all is broken, even ground to pulp.

When I stand here this quiet afternoon I shudder to visualise what is actually happening to millions now and what is going to happen in this period when famine stalks the earth. None can compute what has been called 'the underestimated sum of human pain'. Our supreme task and duty is to guard the homes of the common people from the horrors and miseries of another war. We are all agreed on that.

Our American military colleagues having proclaimed the 'overall strategic concept' and computed available resources, always proceed to the next step – namely, the method. Here again there is widespread agreement. A world organisation has already been erected for the prime purpose of preventing war. UNO the successor of the League of Nations, with the decisive addition of the United States and all that that means, is already at work. We must make sure that its work is fruitful, that it is a reality and not a sham, that it is a force for action, and not merely a frothing of words, that it is a true temple of peace in which the shields of many nations can someday be hung up, and not merely a cockpit in a Tower of Babel. Before we cast away the solid assurances of national armaments for self-preservation we must be certain that our temple is built, not upon shifting sands or quagmires, but upon the rock. Anyone can see with his eyes open that our path will be difficult and also long, but if we persevere together as we did in the two world wars – though not, alas in the interval between them – I cannot doubt that we shall achieve our common purpose in the end.

I have, however, a definite and practical purpose to make for action. Courts and magistrates may be set up but they cannot function without sheriffs and constables. The United Nations Organisation must immediately begin to be equipped with an international armed force. In such a matter we can only go step by step, but we must begin now. I propose that each of the Powers and States should be invited to delegate a certain number of air squadrons to the service of the world organisation. These squadrons would be trained and prepared in their own countries, but would move around in rotation from one country to another. They would wear the uniform of their own countries but with different badges. They would not be required to act against their own nation, but in other respects they would be directed by the world organisation. This might be started on a modest scale and would grow as confidence grew. I wished to see this done after the First World War, and I devoutly trust it may be done forthwith.

It would nevertheless be wrong and imprudent to entrust the secret knowledge or experience of the atomic bomb, which the United States, Great Britain and Canada now share, to the world organisation, while it is still in infancy. It would be criminal madness to cast it adrift in this still agitated and un-united world. No one in any country has slept less well in their beds because this knowledge and the method and the raw materials to apply it are at present largely retained in American hands. I do not believe we should all have slept so soundly had the positions been reversed and if some Communist or neo-Fascist State monopolised for the time being these dread agencies. The fear of them alone might easily have been used to enforce totalitarian systems upon the free democratic world. With consequences appalling to human imagination. God has willed that this shall not be and we have a least a breathing space to set our house in order before this peril has to be encountered: and even then if no effort is spared, we should still possess so formidable a superiority as to impose effective deterrents upon its employment, or threat of employment by others. Ultimately, when the essential brotherhood of man is truly embodied and expressed in a world organisation with all the necessary practical safeguards to make it effective, these powers would naturally be confided to that world organisation.

Now I come to the second danger of these two marauders, which threatens the cottage, the home, and the ordinary people – namely tyranny. We cannot be blind to the fact that the liberties enjoyed by individual citizens throughout the British Empire are not valid in a considerable number of countries, some of which are very powerful. In these States control is enforced upon the common people by various kinds of all-embracing police governments. The power of the State is exercised without restraint, either by dictators or by compact oligarchies operating through a privileged party and a political police. It is not our duty at this time when difficulties are so numerous to interfere forcibly in the internal affairs of countries, which we have not conquered in war. But we must never cease to proclaim in fearless tones the great principles of freedom and the rights of man which are the joint inheritance of the English-speaking world and which through Magna Carta, the Bill of Rights, the Habeas Corpus, trial by jury, and the English common law find their most famous expression in the American Declaration of Independence.

All this means that the people of any country have the right and should have the power by constitutional action, by free unfettered elections, with secret ballot, to choose or change the character or form of government under which they dwell; that freedom of speech and thought should reign; that courts of justice, independent of the executive unbiased by any party should administer laws, which have received the broad assent of large majorities or are consecrated by time and custom. Here are the titled deeds of freedom, which should lie in every cottage home. Here is the message of the British and American peoples to mankind. Let us preach what we practise – let us practise what we preach.

I have now stated the two great dangers, which menace the homes of the people: War and Tyranny. I have not yet spoken of poverty and privation, which are in many cases the prevailing anxiety. But if the dangers of war and tyranny are removed, there is no doubt that science and co-operation can bring in the next few years to the world, certainly in the next few decades newly taught in the sharpening school of war, an expansion of material well-being beyond anything that has yet occurred in human experience. Now, at this sad and breathless moment, we are plunged in the hunger and distress which are the aftermath of our stupendous struggle; but this will pass and may pass quickly, and there is no reason except human folly of sub-human crime which should deny to all the nations the inauguration and enjoyment of an age of plenty. I have often used words, which I learned fifty years ago from a great Irish-American orator, a friend of mine, Mr Bourke Cockran. 'There is enough for all. The earth is a generous mother; she will provide in plentiful abundance food for all her children if they will but cultivate her soil in justice and in peace.' So far I feel that we are in full agreement.

Now, while still pursuing the method of realising our overall strategic concept, I come to the crux of what I have travelled here to say. Neither the sure prevention of war, nor the continuous rise of world organisation will be gained without what I have called the fraternal association of the English-speaking peoples. This means a special relationship between the British Commonwealth and Empire and the United States. This is no time for generalities, and I will venture to be precise. Fraternal association requires not only the growing friendship and mutual understanding between our two vast but kindred systems of society, but the continuance of the intimate relationship between our military advisers, leading to common study of potential dangers, the similarity of weapons and manuals of instructions, and to the interchange of officers and cadets at technical colleges. It should carry with it the continuance of the present facilities for mutual security by the joint use of all Naval and Air Force bases in the possession of either country all over the world. This would perhaps double the mobility of the American Navy and Air Force. It would greatly expand that of the British Empire Forces and it might well lead, if and as the world calms down, to important financial savings. Already we use together a large number of islands; more may well be entrusted to our joint care in the near future.

The United States has already a Permanent Defence Agreement with the Dominion of Canada, which is so devotedly attached to the British Commonwealth and Empire. This Agreement is more effective than many of those which have often been made under formal alliances. This principle should be extended to all British Commonwealths with full reciprocity. Thus, whatever happens, and thus only, shall we be secure ourselves and able to work together for the high and simple causes that are dear to us and bode no ill to any. Eventually there may come – I feel eventually there will come – the principle of common citizenship, but that we may be content to leave to destiny, whose outstretched arm many of us can already clearly see.

There is however an important question we must ask ourselves. Would a special relationship between the United States and the British Commonwealth be inconsistent with our over-riding loyalties to the World Organisation? I reply that, on the contrary, it is probably the only means by which that organisation will achieve its full stature and strength. There are already the special United States relations with Canada which I have just mentioned, and there are the special relations between the United States and the South American Republics. We British have our twenty years Treaty of Collaboration and Mutual Assistance with Soviet Russia. I agree with Mr Bevin, the Foreign Secretary of Great Britain, that it might well be a fifty years Treaty so far as we are concerned. We aim at nothing but mutual assistance and collaboration. The British have an alliance with Portugal unbroken since 1384, and which produced fruitful results at critical moments in the late war. None of these clash with the general interest of a world agreement, or a world organisation; on the contrary they help it. 'In my father's house are many mansions.' Special associations between members of the United Nations which have no aggressive point against any other country, which harbour no design incompatible with the Charter of the United Nations, far from being harmful, are beneficial and, as I believe, indispensable.

I spoke earlier of the Temple of Peace. Workmen from all countries must build that temple. If two of the workmen know each other particularly well and are old friends, if their families are inter-mingled, and if they have 'faith in each other's purpose, hope in each other's future and charity towards each other's shortcomings' – to quote some good words I read here the other day – why cannot they work together at the common task as friends and partners? Why cannot they share their tools and thus increase each other's working powers? Indeed they must do so or else the temple may not be built, or, being built, it may collapse, and we shall all be proved again unteachable and have to go and try to learn again for a third time in a school of war, incomparably more rigorous than that from which we have just been released. The dark ages may return, the Stone Age may return on the gleaming wings of science, and what might now shower immeasurable material blessings upon mankind may even bring about its total destruction. Beware, I say; time may be short. Do not let us take the course of allowing events to drift along until it is too late. If there is to be a fraternal association of the kind I have described, with all the extra strength and security which both our countries can derive from it, let us make sure that that great fact is known to the world, and that it plays its part in steadying and stabilising the foundations of peace. There is the path of wisdom. Prevention is better than cure.

A shadow has fallen upon the scenes so lately lighted by the Allied victory. Nobody knows what Soviet Russia and its

Communist international organisation intends to do in the immediate future, or what are the limits, if any, to their expansive and proselytising tendencies. I have a strong admiration and regard for the valiant Russian people and for my wartime comrade, Marshal Stalin. There is deep sympathy and goodwill in Britain – and I doubt not here also – towards the peoples of all the Russias and a resolve to persevere through many differences and rebuffs in establishing lasting friendships. We understand the Russian need to be secure on her western frontiers by the removal of all possibility of German aggression. We welcome Russia to her rightful place among the leading nations of the world. We welcome her flag upon the seas. Above all, we welcome constant, frequent and growing contacts between the Russian people and our own people on both sides of the Atlantic. It is my duty however, for I am sure you would wish me to state the facts as I see them to you, to place before you certain facts about the present position in Europe.

From Stettin in the Baltic to Trieste in the Adriatic, an iron curtain has descended across the Continent. Behind that line lie all the capitals of the ancient states of Central and Eastern Europe. Warsaw, Berlin, Prague, Vienna, Budapest, Belgrade, Bucharest and Sofia, all these famous cities and the populations around them lie in what I must call the Soviet sphere, and all are subject in one form or another, not only to Soviet influence but to a very high and, in many cases, increasing measure of control from Moscow. Athens alone – Greece with its immortal glories – is free to decide its future at an election under British, American and French observation. The Russian-dominated Polish Government has been encouraged to make enormous and wrongful inroads upon Germany, and mass expulsions of millions of Germans on a scale grievous and undreamed-of are now taking place. The Communist parties, which were very small in all these Eastern States of Europe, have been raised to pre-eminence and power far beyond their numbers and are seeking everywhere to obtain totalitarian control. Police governments are prevailing in nearly every case, and so far, except in Czechoslovakia, there is no true democracy.

Turkey and Persia are both profoundly alarmed and disturbed at the claims which are being made upon them and at the pressure being exerted by the Moscow Government. An attempt is being made by the Russians in Berlin to build up a quasi-Communist party in their zone of Occupied Germany by showing special favours to groups of left-wing German leaders. At the end of the fighting last June, the American and British Armies withdrew westwards, in accordance with an earlier agreement, to a depth at some points of 150 miles upon a front of nearly four hundred miles, in order to allow our Russian allies to occupy this vast expanse of territory which the Western Democracies had conquered.

If now the Soviet Government tries, by separate action, to build up a pro-Communist Germany in their areas, this will cause new serious difficulties in the British and American zones, and will give the defeated Germans the power of putting themselves up to auction between the Soviets and the Western Democracies. Whatever conclusions may be drawn from these facts – and facts they are – this is certainly not the Liberated Europe we fought to build up. Nor is it one which contains the essentials of permanent peace.

The safety of the world requires a new unity in Europe, from which no nation should be permanently outcast. It is from the quarrels of the strong parent races in Europe that the world wars we have witnessed, or which occurred in former times, have sprung. Twice in our own lifetime we have seen the United States, against their wishes and their traditions, against arguments, the force of which it is impossible not to comprehend, drawn by irresistible forces, into these wars in time to secure the victory of the good cause, but only after frightful slaughter and devastation had occurred. Twice the United States has had to send several millions of its young men across the Atlantic to find the war; but now war can find any nation, wherever it may dwell between dusk and dawn. Surely we should work with conscious purpose for a grand pacification of Europe, within the structure of the United Nations and in accordance with its Charter. That I feel is an open cause of policy of very great importance.

In front of the iron curtain which lies across Europe are other causes for anxiety. In Italy the Communist Party is seriously hampered by having to support the Communist-trained Marshal Tito's claims to former Italian territory at the head of the Adriatic. Nevertheless the future of Italy hangs in the balance. Again one cannot imagine a regenerated Europe without a strong France. All my public life I have worked for a strong France and I never lost faith in her destiny, even in the darkest hours. I will not lose faith now. However, in a great number of countries, far from the Russian frontiers and throughout the world, Communist fifth columns are established and work in complete unity and absolute obedience to the directions they receive from the Communist centre. Except in the British Commonwealth and in the United States where Communism is in its infancy, the Communist parties or fifth columns constitute a growing challenge and peril to Christian civilisation. These are sombre facts for anyone to have to recite on the morrow of a victory gained by so much splendid comradeship in arms and in the cause of freedom and democracy; but we should be most unwise not to face them squarely while time remains.

The outlook is also anxious in the Far East and especially in

Manchuria. The Agreement which was made at Yalta, to which I was a party, was extremely favourable to Soviet Russia, but it was made at a time when no one could say that the German war might not extend all through the summer and autumn of 1945 and when the Japanese war was expected to last for a further 18 months from the end of the German war. In this country you are all so well-informed about the Far East, and such devoted friends of China, that I do not need to expatiate on the situation there.

I have felt bound to portray the shadow which, alike in the west and in the east, falls upon the world. I was a high minister at the time of the Versailles Treaty and a close friend of Mr Lloyd George, who was the head of the British delegation at Versailles. I did not myself agree with many things that were done, but I have a very strong impression in my mind of that situation, and I find it painful to contrast it with that which prevails now. In those days there were high hopes and unbounded confidence that the wars were over, and that the League of Nations would become all-powerful. I do not see or feel that same confidence or even the same hopes in the haggard world at the present time.

On the other hand I repulse the idea that a new war is inevitable; still more that it is imminent. It is because I am sure that our fortunes are still in our own hands and that we hold the power to save the future, that I feel the duty to speak out now that I have the occasion and the opportunity to do so. I do not believe that Soviet Russia desires war. What they desire is the fruits of war and the indefinite expansion of their power and doctrines. But what we have to consider here today while time remains, is the permanent prevention of war and the establishment of conditions of freedom and democracy as rapidly as possible in all countries. Our difficulties and dangers will not be removed by closing our eyes to them. They will not be removed by mere waiting to see what happens; nor will they be removed by a policy of appeasement. What is needed is a settlement, and the longer this is delayed, the more difficult it will be and the greater our dangers will become.

From what I have seen of our Russian friends and Allies during the war, I am convinced that there is nothing they admire so much as strength, and there is nothing for which they have less respect than for weakness, especially military weakness. For that reason the old doctrine of a balance of power is unsound. We cannot afford, if we can help it, to work on narrow margins, offering temptations to a trial of strength. If the Western Democracies stand together in strict adherence to the principles of the United Nations Charter, their influence for furthering those principles will be immense and no one is likely to molest them. If however they become divided or falter in their duty and if these all-important years are allowed to slip away then indeed catastrophe may overwhelm us all.

Last time I saw it all coming and cried aloud to my own fellow-countrymen and to the world, but no one paid any attention. Up till the year 1933 or even 1935, Germany might have been saved from the awful fate which has overtaken her and we might all have been spared the miseries Hitler let loose upon mankind. There never was a war in all history easier to prevent by timely action than the one which has just desolated such great areas of the globe. It could have been prevented in my belief without the firing of a single shot, and Germany might be powerful, prosperous and honoured to-day; but no one would listen and one by one we were all sucked into the awful whirlpool. We surely must not let that happen again. This can only be achieved by reaching now, in 1946, a good understanding on all points with Russia under the general authority of the United Nations Organisation and by the maintenance of that good understanding through many peaceful years, by the world instrument, supported by the whole strength of the English-speaking world and all its connections. There is the solution which I respectfully offer to you in this Address to which I have given the title 'The Sinews of Peace'.

Let no man underrate the abiding power of the British Empire and Commonwealth. Because you see the 46 millions in our island harassed about their food supply, of which they only grow one half, even in war-time, or because we have difficulty in restarting our industries and export trade after six years of passionate war effort, do not suppose that we shall not come through these dark years of privation as we have come through the glorious years of agony, or that half a century from now, you will not see 70 or 80 millions of Britons spread about the world and united in defence of our traditions, our way of life, and of the world causes which you and we espouse. If the population of the English-speaking Commonwealths be added to that of the United States with all that such co-operation implies in the air, on the sea, all over the globe and in science and in industry, and in moral force, there will be no quivering, precarious balance of power to offer its temptation to ambition or adventure. On the contrary, there will be an overwhelming assurance of security. If we adhere faithfully to the Charter of the United Nations and walk forward in sedate and sober strength seeking no one's land or treasure, seeking to lay no arbitrary control upon the thoughts of men; if all British moral and material forces and convictions are joined with your own in fraternal association, the high-roads of the future will be clear, not only for us but for all, not only for our time, but for a century to come.

PART IV

'It hasn't half kicked up a shindig'

Reactions I

Writing to her parents immediately after Churchill's return to Washington, Jo Sturdee allowed herself a political judgement. 'I feel it was or will be proved in the future to be quite a historic speech, although it hasn't half kicked up a shindig here.'[1]

The opposition to the speech would traverse the world. The initial storm of protest came in the United States – first in the media and then on the streets of New York. Predictably it also came from the Roosevelt family. Then the president, Truman, would distance himself from the speech and at a press conference on 8 March repeatedly deny that he had known in advance what Churchill would say – a lie that risked public refutation. He even insisted that his presence next to Churchill on the gymnasium platform did not indicate any endorsement of the speech – a distortion that was not only untrue, but was revealed as such because Pathé News showed him applauding the parts of the speech that mattered. To add insult to injury he then forbade Dean Acheson, the Undersecretary of State, from attending Churchill's final speech in New York before his return to Southampton, as well as the reception scheduled for the day prior to his return sailing.

The second wave of protest emanated predictably from Moscow. Stalin broke every precedent and gave an interview to *Pravda*

which lasted through four days. The attack was personal and ideo-
logical. Churchill was a warmonger, in his own way as much a
racist as Adolf Hitler, an inveterate opponent of the Bolshevik
Revolution, and the *New York Times* headlined the interview
'Stalin says Churchill stirs war and flouts Anglo-Russian Pact'. It
was a violent, vehement outpouring of Stalin's dismay and anger.
He had not foreseen Churchill's attack. He would not forgive it.
Fulton was an arrow that pierced Stalin's armour and he felt the
blow.

Finally came the British reaction – much cooler but politically
far more dangerous to Churchill. At Westminster the Conservative
Backbench Foreign Affairs Committee gave some support but
urged that 'far more has been read into the Fulton Speech both by
opponents and by over-enthusiastic friends than Churchill
intended to convey'.[2]

Ominously, *The Times*, close to the Conservative Party, wrote of
the 'perhaps less happy' passages in his speech.[3]

Waiting disconsolately in the wings was Anthony Eden,
surrounded by others in the Tory Party who felt the time had more
than come for Churchill to step aside and become the elder
statesman 'concentrating', as Eden actually suggests, 'on grand
speeches on grand themes', reflecting his own views rather than the
policies of the opposition. All these signs and sounds of discontent
were to be rebuffed by the return of the rejuvenated Churchill to
Britain but until then London's reaction was dangerous.

Lord Halifax of course reflected the dismay of likeminded
Tories, as it did his own predilection for what Churchill saw as
appeasement. Having returned from Miami for a few days in the
sun after his speech in Fulton, Churchill received a telegram from
Halifax urging him to say that his Fulton speech had been misrep-
resented. It arrived four days after Stalin's tirade and urged

Churchill to apologise to 'Uncle Joe'. He responded that this reminded him of the advice he received before the war that he should visit Adolf Hitler and – as was implied – apologise for his bellicose opposition to the dictator. Churchill rejected Halifax's advice but refrained from reminding him that, back in May 1940, Halifax had urged mediating with Hitler via Mussolini.

In his *Life of Lord Halifax*, the Earl of Birkenhead quotes Halifax's telegram to Churchill: 'Uncle Joe's speech is pretty insolent but any public argument between you will get the world nowhere except in a worse temper.' Halifax urged Churchill to say publicly that 'Uncle Joe has completely misunderstood' Fulton; 'Uncle Joe does not appear to appreciate any of the causes that are responsible for the present anxiety about Russian policy'; and then crucially, 'You attach too much importance to your war comradeship with Uncle Joe to be willing to allow it to be frosted over if it can be avoided.' Birkenhead rightly notes that for Churchill this could have only one meaning: 'It must have seemed like some resurrection from the past, another indication of that incapacity for righteous anger in the face of evil that had been the fraud of appeasement.'[4]

Birkenhead then recounts a fascinating phone call from Churchill to Halifax's wife Dorothy, after he had received Halifax's telegram. He said to her that he could not possibly follow Halifax's proposal, which had included the idea that Churchill should visit Uncle Joe after his departure from the USA. It would, Churchill said, be like 'the whipped cur coming to heel – like going to see Hitler just before the war'.

Equally telling is Halifax's reaction to Churchill's anger. As his biographer notes, he 'had a thick skin on the subject and was in no way mortified'.[5] Indeed, Halifax's rejection of Churchill's attitude was characteristically blunt: 'I thought at the time as I have thought since, that he was wrong.' Halifax wanted to mediate in 1940, and he wanted to do so again in 1946,

I will return in more detail to both the American and Soviet criticisms of Fulton, but first it is important to consider just why Churchill's speech stirred up such upset in the United States.

There was the matter of the Bomb. In his Fulton speech Churchill carefully ruled out any idea of sharing nuclear technology with the United Nations Organisation or its peace force, and this clearly implied that it should not be made available to the Russians. Churchill and Truman would both be aware of Stalin's frantic efforts to catch up on the Bomb both by espionage and the manic pace of research in the USSR supervised by the KGB boss, Beria.

The technology Churchill describes as being held by the USA, the UK and Canada in his Fulton speech masked both the truth and British resentment. Churchill knew that 'Britain had now been cut out of the atomic bomb project and that the Combined Chiefs of Staff were withering away. This was the background of his speech.'[6] Fulton does speak about shared bases and logistical co-operation. But it does not refer to the co-operation the British most wanted. They wanted what they saw as their share of America's atomic secrets. On this, Churchill, Bevin and Attlee had left the US government in no doubt that there was to be no 'give' on the UK side.

On 29 August 1940, despite Churchill's reservations, a small black metal box had been shipped out of Liverpool to New York containing 'Britain's technological crown jewels' including plans for the atom bomb.[7] By handing over its atomic secrets, Britain had earned, in Churchill's view, inclusion in the American nuclear programme. To be excluded now was an offence as deep in its way as Roosevelt's snubbing Churchill over Stalin. Ultimately America's attitude on sharing its nuclear secrets would lead to Prime Minister Attlee's unilateral decision to build Britain's own bomb. Bevin, Britain's foreign secretary, resented being talked at and down to by Secretary of State Byrnes. Bevin argued defiantly over the need for a British nuclear weapon: 'we have got to have this thing over here whatever it costs and . . . we've got to have the bloody Union Jack flying on top of it'.[8]

The Americans would have seen Fulton's call for the closest alliance between the United States and Britain as coming danger- ously close to a demand for the nuclear intimacy they were determined not to grant.

There was also the sheer heresy of depicting Stalin and his Soviet empire as the new 'marauder' threatening tyranny, if not war. It is hard to imagine the veneration felt at that time for Stalin and, above all, for the courage of the Russian people. What was happening behind the Iron Curtain was little known and little reported. What is more, most people did not want to know. It was complicated, foreign, a long distance away and the GIs, their families and loved ones were focused on life back home.

In August the previous year, Truman had called for universal military training. Congress would have none of it and overwhelm- ingly defeated the proposal. Public opinion in Fulton, however, was, as reported, firmly anti-isolationist but its citizens, like the vast majority of Americans, were allergic to foreign entangle- ments. In calling for an ever-closer military alliance in the face of the Soviets, Churchill at Fulton was arguing against the grain of American opinion and with an administration still deeply uncer- tain and electorally weak. Truman was an unexpected president and, compared with the monumental Roosevelt, seemingly polit- ically puny. In Fulton, the president cut a grand figure but not to the nation as a whole. As we know, he had not as yet been directly elected. Truman's position was also ambiguous on foreign policy. Marshall was not yet at his side and he did not trust Byrnes. The fact was that Truman was still listening to the voices that had surrounded Roosevelt. After Potsdam he had sent Harry Hopkins, one of his closest advisors, to Moscow to assure Stalin that the USA and he 'had no ambitions in Eastern Europe' and that America's only interests 'concerned world peace'. Hopkins had returned, 'bubbling with enthusiasm about Soviet friendliness'. He assured the president that 'Stalin will co-operate'.[9]

And then there were the emphases so vital to Churchill's purpose, the passages that go to the heart of his judgement and determination: that the United Kingdom, the United States and Canada should not share the secrets of the atomic bomb with anyone; that the British Empire and Commonwealth retain an 'abiding power'[10] that no man should underrate; that the special relationship between Britain and the United States could contain the Soviet threat; that that threat was evident and growing as Russia 'desired the indefinite expansion of their power and doctrines'[11]; that an Iron Curtain had fallen across Europe from Stettin in the Baltic to Trieste in the Adriatic, behind which their grip was ever tightening; and that – and this was the first time he had raised this spectre – the Russians in Berlin were seeking 'to build up a pro-Communist Germany in their areas', which would cause serious difficulties in the British and American zones.

Lastly, while there was daring in Churchill's appeal there was also effrontery, even impertinence. Here was an ousted British prime minister who had come to the United States to plead for a loan, calmly lecturing America on the responsibilities of power. It was, he proclaimed at Fulton, 'a solemn moment for American Democracy. Viewing the world they should not rest on their laurels – you must feel not only the sense of duty done but also anxiety lest you fall below the level of achievement.'[12]

It was breath-taking in its temerity. This was not merely playing Greece to Rome, namely the more cultured nation advising the more powerful. This was Greece telling Rome what it had to do.

In the light of all this, the harshness of the US media reaction was understandable and, for Truman, probably predictable. To the *Chicago Sun* Churchill's aim was nothing less than 'world domination through arms by the United States and the British Empire'. The more measured and authoritative *Wall Street Journal* condemned the speech and reminded Churchill and the British that 'the US wants no alliance or anything that resembles an alliance with any other nation'. Behind its disapproval lay not only the suspicion of entanglement but also the self-confidence that the USA, at its peak of power, didn't need any alliance. Another paper, *The Nation*, accused Churchill of adding 'poison' to a deteriorating relationship with the USSR. It also charged Truman with ineptitude in having sat on the platform next to Churchill at Fulton.

It was no doubt criticism of this order that led Truman, a few days later at a press conference, to explicitly deny that his presence implied endorsement. Even more shamingly he repeatedly denied that he had seen the speech before, read it, or known of its contents.

With Ike to Richmond

With all the drama of Churchill's visit to the United States in the first three months of 1946, 8 March was to prove one of the most dramatic days. It was on this day that Truman and Byrnes were to deny publicly, not once but repeatedly, that they had known what Churchill would say at Fulton. Churchill was perhaps not surprised but nonetheless dismayed. Back in London he would complain that the Pathé newsreel proved that Truman had applauded all the most 'controversial' passages in his speech.

The press conference on the 8th was given by both the president and the secretary of state. As the *Daily Telegraph* reported, 'In spite of persistent questioning Mr Truman declined to be drawn into making any direct comment on Mr Churchill's speech at Fulton on Tuesday. He insisted that he had not read the speech in advance.' The tone adopted by Byrnes was slightly defensive but equally deceptive. He stated that 'he had not known before Mr Churchill's speech what Britain's former Prime Minister intended to say. He had seen Mr Churchill three weeks before but the speech had not been written at that time.' In fact, as we know from Churchill's cable to Bevin sent the day before, Churchill was emphatic that he 'showed it albeit an earlier draft to Mr Byrnes the night before leaving Washington'. Churchill adds of Byrnes that 'he was excited about it and did not suggest any alterations'.[1]

The 8th also proved dramatic because of Churchill's visit to Richmond and Williamsburg in Virginia. He was accompanied by Eisenhower and the visit was the scene of an accident that was certainly dangerous and might even have proved fatal. It was also the occasion of intensive discussions between the two men, a proposal from the general and a shared experience of popular acclaim that would have enhanced their taste for public office.

The accident occurred during the second half of the visit. The day's timetable had been meticulously choreographed. On arrival in Richmond from Washington both men alighted and were driven in an open car to the Capitol where the speeches were made. There were 150,000 people on the streets of the city, once the Confederate capital. The journey took twenty-five minutes. It was raining but this did nothing to dampen the enthusiasm of the crowds. The American media's disapproval of the Fulton speech did not appear to be replicated, and Truman's distancing at his press conference would not yet have been known to people. Churchill enjoyed himself 'acknowledging the cheers with his V sign'. On his arrival at the Capitol the military cadets lined up at the front where they, although 'drenched, snapped smartly to attention'.

Inside he was welcomed by William Tuck, the state governor, and he soon settled into his speech. His tone was designed to mollify the opposition Fulton had aroused. He had the audience in mirth as he joked about the furore he had caused. Did they not think, Churchill asked, 'they were running some risk by inviting him to talk to them?' No they did not. Any tension felt by the Virginia Assembly was dissipated. What is more he chided the media for suggesting that the president's presence on the stage at Fulton indicated that he was 'partly responsible' for its content. No – he had been speaking for himself.[2]

In the main body of his speech to the Assembly, Churchill never referred to the 'Iron Curtain', or even to Russia. His message was unthreatening and dignified. 'In these last years of my life there is a message of which I conceive myself to be the bearer. It is that we should stand together in malice towards none, in greed for nothing but in defence of those causes which we hold dear.'[3] Referring back to his address to Congress in 1941, Britain and America ought 'to walk together in majesty and peace'. He was certain that was the wish 'of an overwhelming majority of 200,000,000 Britons and Americans'. Churchill quoted John Bunyan's *Pilgrim's Progress*: 'Great heart must have his sword and armour to guard the pilgrims on their way.'[4] But what he offered and wanted above all was 'a union of hearts based on conviction and common ideals . . . Both countries must find a means and a method of working together not only in times of war but in times of peace.' This was to elicit a proposal afterwards from the ever practical Eisenhower. Churchill didn't want Britain to become the 49th state, nor America to rejoin the British Empire, but to pave 'a path of wisdom' between such 'scarecrow extremes'. Peace could not be preserved by casting aside 'our panoply of warlike strength', he warned, perhaps thinking above all of US demobilisation and exodus from Europe as well as the cessation of the close collaboration between the US and British chiefs of staff achieved during the war.[5]

Churchill displayed his skill in flattering an audience that mattered – again and again hitting exactly the right note both for the delegates and for Eisenhower. The Virginia Assembly was the successor of 'the most ancient law making body on the main land of the Western hemisphere'[6] – the descendant of the House of Burgesses established by the Jamestown settlers who had arrived in 1607. Here he was beside Eisenhower, whose qualities he compared to Robert E. Lee, the commander of the Confederate

Army. As a younger man Churchill had studied the Virginia battle-fields of the Civil War. He confided that in the Second World War he had read secret German reports referring to 'those ridiculous American troops'. 'Well,' he growled, to rapturous applause, 'surely they should not have forgotten or have ignored so soon the example of tenacity, will power and self-devotion which shines all through the records of the great American Civil War.'[7]

Churchill now turned to Eisenhower who, more than any other, had worked to weld Allied troops – British, American, Canadian – 'into a force which fought as soldiers of a single nation'.[8]

Churchill sat down to thunderous applause. The Speaker of the Assembly then introduced General Eisenhower, who had not planned to speak but the delegates insisted. 'I could not come on a happier occasion than as one of the aides of one of the great men of the world . . . Of all the things that supported me in the years of war none was so inspiring as the courage and indomitable spirit of the Prime Minister of Great Britain.'[9]

They left the Capitol on a wave of enthusiasm. Eisenhower spoke individually to GIs who served in France and their warmth was overwhelming. Clearly he was popular on a scale of intensity that impressed Churchill. Back in 1944, when Churchill was mired in disagreement with Roosevelt, Eisenhower had confided that after the war he would retire from the military and devote himself 'to the promoting of good US–British relations'.[10]

Eisenhower did, in fact, retire from politics to become president of Columbia University but then decided, a few years later, to return to politics, run for president and win. It is a conjecture but the adulation both men experienced in 1946 may have contributed to the decision of both to run for the highest offices their countries could afford.

Fate, however, might have frustrated all ambitions later that afternoon. Leaving Richmond by train they travelled the short distance to Williamsburg – the old colonial capital meticulously restored by the Rockefeller family. John D. Rockefeller Jr. would join them for dinner. First, however, they were to tour Williamsburg in an open horse-drawn carriage. This they did but the two horses, frightened by the mass of flash photography, reared up, backing the coach into an iron railing. The harness snapped. As the local paper reported, it was 'a potentially grave accident followed by a hectic scene of confusion and consternation'. In the event neither former cavalry officer panicked. Churchill continued to puff a large black cigar and Eisenhower reached over and regained control of the harness. Churchill's wife, Clementine, surveying the scene, said of her husband only that 'he is good driver. They will be alright.' However, the tour was abandoned.

So they returned to Washington that night. By then both would have been aware of Truman's press conference. The next reaction would come from Moscow. Richmond provided a breathing space and a chance to cement the relationship with Eisenhower but the drama of Churchill's American journey was far from over.

Leaving the Big Apple

Churchill's last ten days in America were based in New York and, in terms of public performance, focused on his concluding speech at the Waldorf Astoria Hotel scheduled for 15 March. It would be attended by over 2,000 guests. On the platform no fewer than forty ambassadors to the United States would take their seats. However, two critically important VIPS were not there: Dean Acheson, the US secretary of state, had been instructed by the president not to attend since 'Urgent matters made it imperative for him to remain in Washington.'[1] The other empty space was predictably that of the other superpower: Andrei Gromyko, then Soviet ambassador, who told the press, 'I do not know anything about it. If my radio set is in good order I will listen.'[2]

These two representatives of the world's two most powerful countries would not be present but both would be totally alert to what Churchill would say. Truman had already distanced himself from Fulton. Stalin was about to launch his counter-offensive.

Stalin's attack on Churchill came in *Pravda* on 14 March. It was virtually unprecedented. Stalin very rarely gave interviews even to the media he controlled. It sought to position Churchill as the aggressor – the instigator of what would be termed the Cold War. It also sought to tar Churchill with a Hitlerian brush by implying that his Anglo-American alliance was racist. Not only that but

Stalin's interview sought to deride the democratic credentials so treasured by Britain and the USA, the absence of which they so deplored in his takeover of Central and Eastern Europe. Roy Jenkins, in his biography of Churchill, rates the 'racist' charge as a 'shrewd hit' but it is difficult to see why. Stalin said to *Pravda*, 'Churchill is starting his process of unleashing war like Hitler with a racial theory declaring that only people who speak English are full blooded nations whose vocation is to control the fate of the whole world.'[3] But a shared language was hardly a blood characteristic.

Jenkins describes Stalin's diatribe against Britain's democratic credentials as 'purely dialectical' and a 'spirited piece of Alice Through the Looking Glass audacity'.[4] Stalin's taunt was this: 'In England today the government of one party is ruling. The Opposition is deprived of the right to take part in the government.' Churchill claims that this is 'true democracy' while in Poland, Romania, Yugoslavia, Bulgaria and Hungary the governments are from four to six parties. This Churchill dismisses as 'totalitarianism, tyranny, a police state'.[5]

There is some debate even today about whether Stalin ruled out any form of democracy in Eastern Europe. Was his adherence to the Yalta protocols pure hypocrisy? Anne Applebaum, in her magisterial account of the Iron Curtain, argues that 'both the Soviet Union and its allies in Eastern Europe thought that democracy would work in their favour'.[6] But what form of democracy? Not the word but the reality. Subsequent events do show that Churchill was not exaggerating and that Stalin was deceiving.

For Churchill, preparing his final major speech of his American tour was an imminent critical test of Stalin's intent. It was to draw attention to the pace of Russian aggression over Iran and Turkey – the focus of so much discussion on the train journey to Missouri. He was to write into his last New York speech a direct challenge to

Stalin. The USA and UK had left Iran as agreed at Tehran by Roosevelt, Stalin and himself. 'But now we are told that the Soviet government, instead of leaving, are actually sending in more troops.' So what was to happen? The 2 March deadline for withdrawal from Iran had come and gone and there had been no Soviet withdrawal.

After the fall of the USSR and the opening of their archives it became known that in 1945 Stalin had pinned a new map on the wall of his dacha and had told Molotov, pointing south of the Caucusus with the stem of his pipe, that 'this frontier I don't like at all . . . the Dardanelles . . . We also have claims to Turkish territory and to Libya.'[7]

Churchill could only speculate on Stalin's ambitions but his conviction, stated clearly at Fulton and to be repeated now in New York, was that if the West did not resist Stalin would always go for the most he could get. Strength was all he would respect. So Churchill was clear that the USS *Missouri*'s mission to Istanbul was critical. He was right. Churchill would sail from New York on 20 March. Two days later the USS *Missouri* left New York for Istanbul. On that same day, 22 March, Russia conceded and announced its troops would leave Iran. This came too late for Churchill's finale at the Waldorf Astoria but it did prove his point as London and Washington acknowledged. Although Churchill's departure from New York would see the fiercest demonstrations and criticisms of his message at Fulton, history had reached a tipping point and Fulton was on the way to historic vindication.

His last days in New York equalled the drama of the rest of his trip.

First there was Stalin's attack in *Pravda* on the 14th. Then there was a further chorus of American criticism. In the House of Representatives Howard Buffet, a Republican, charged Churchill with wishing to 'entangle the USA in another war'.[8] Churchill, he said on US radio networks, was 'war-mongering'. Howard Buffet was from the isolationist right. From the other side of the House, the Democratic Secretary of Commerce urged his country to return to its traditional policy of 'mediating between British and Russian interests'[9] and refrain from aligning with either. The Secretary of Commerce was speaking at a dinner on the 14th held in honour of, and in the presence of, Roosevelt's widow, Eleanor. Meanwhile one of their sons, James, joined the attack on Churchill from Chicago over the radio. He charged that 'The kind of speeches Mr. Churchill has been making in this country are harmful to the peace of the world.'[10] Meanwhile in his suite in the Waldorf Astoria Churchill was preparing for his final speech of the tour scheduled to take place in the same hotel.

On board the *Queen Mary*, the 81,000 ton liner preparing to take him home, workmen were frantically trying to complete alterations to the principal passenger suite on the main deck amidships. As the *Daily Telegraph* reported, 'As a gesture to Mr. Churchill for his outstanding service to the country, Cunard are fitting out this suite with something like its pre-war comfort.'[11]

As to his official agenda on his journey – the British loan – Churchill felt he had done his best and was now content to leave the outcome to Congress. He had further meetings with Bernard Baruch and cabled to Attlee that he was confident Baruch would not now oppose action on the loan though he was still against it. However, 'he considers that the Russian situation makes it essential that our countries should stand together'. Churchill was trying to lever his 'other agenda' to advance the official one.

He also made time to give another sitting to Douglas Chandor – a British painter – to complete the portrait of the 'Big Three' meeting at Yalta. He was depicted in his RAF uniform but he wanted all his decorations painted in – including ones he had not brought with him. It was important to him that his image as a military leader in the Second World War was retained. After all, neither Roosevelt nor President Truman were ever depicted in uniform.

It was wet on 15 March. His speech would be in the evening. Beforehand, he would ride in an open car to City Hall to receive New York's Gold Medal. Along the route 1,400 police were posted and, despite the weather, Churchill rode resplendent in the grey-green Chrysler that had once carried the king and queen. He sported his black homburg hat and a white silk muffler against the elements. The protesting amongst the crowds appeared to elate him. They were outnumbered by thousands shouting 'Good old Winnie'. In all over 750,000 people were on the streets to watch the ticker-tape parade. However at the City Hall Plaza those most antagonistic suddenly caught the cameras waving placards proclaiming, 'No American shall die for Churchill – No World War III'.[12]

Inside City Hall a police band played the national anthems and, for good measure, the police glee club gave a rendering of 'There'll always be an England'. Flatteringly, if inaccurately, the citation on his gold medal read 'To the Rt. Hon Winston S Churchill victorious Prime Minister of the British Empire'.

Churchill was in his element and ready for his final speech at the Waldorf Astoria. Neither Acheson nor Gromyko would be there but, rather like Kennan's 'long telegram' they had asked for it and they were going to get it. Unlike his speech at Richmond, Churchill was not out to mollify. Perhaps he felt there was no longer any need. The day before – the day of Stalin's onslaught – he had received a most private note from Truman. It read simply, if still guardedly: 'The people in Missouri were highly pleased with your visit and enjoyed what you had to say.'[13]

In the event, Churchill was absolutely unapologetic. On Fulton he said:

> I do not wish to withdraw or modify a single word. If men who 'hold all the 180 million Russians and many more millions outside Russia in their grip' discourage or chill Western efforts to ensure their honoured place in the van of world organisation . . . the responsibility will be entirely theirs.[14]

Churchill was presaging the outmanoeuvring of Stalin by the Marshall Plan and the re-establishment of the German economy. On Russia he concluded: 'There is no reason why Soviet Russia should feel unrewarded for her efforts in the war. If her losses have been grievous her gains have been magnificent.'

He was going to add another paragraph to his speech but at the last moment deleted it. It would have said of Stalin's denunciation of Fulton:

> It is extraordinary that the head of a mighty, victorious government should descend . . . to enter into personal controversy with a man who has no official position of any kind. Nor am I dismayed by harsh words – even from the most powerful of dictators. Indeed I had years of it from Hitler and managed to get along alright.[15]

It is a pity the paragraph was deleted as it would have been a fitting response to Stalin's attempt to compare Churchill's enthusiasm for the English-speaking world with Hitler's advocacy of Aryan racial mastery. There may have been 2,000 demonstrators picketing the Waldorf Astoria that night waving placards denouncing him: 'Churchill wants war. We want peace.' But Churchill knew he had won the argument. He was ready to bid farewell to the Big Apple.

Homecoming

The last hours before sailing on 20 March gave Clementine Churchill and their daughter a little time for shopping. The two women watched the St Patrick's Day Parade on 5th Avenue. Churchill stayed at the Waldorf Astoria and savoured the generosity of American friends. The Metropolitan Club of New York had sent him a hundred of the very finest cigars presented in a handsome humidor. Another gift was that of a century-old silver cigar case. His preferences were known and indulged.

Boarding the *Queen Mary*, Churchill was delighted that Captain Ford was in command. He had been a commodore of conveys at the height of the Battle of the Atlantic and Churchill was to spend many hours on the bridge reliving that struggle by Admiral Doenitz's U-boats to break the trans-Atlantic bridge. Churchill had always seen it as the most crucial campaign for Britain. If the bridge had been severed in 1942 Britain might have starved. If it had not been reinforced and so strengthened by a combination of the code breakers' success at Bletchley Park, the invention of new depth charge technology and the closure of the mid-Atlantic gap by new long-distance aircraft, then the build-up before D-Day would have been rendered impossible. Unlike the westward voyage on the *Queen Elizabeth* there is no record of any speech to the crew and others on board and the ship would have been far less full – there were no US troops going to Europe, only GIs preparing for the return voyage and repatriation from Europe. Yet Churchill would have been delighted by the success of the east-ward bound USS *Missouri* following two days behind. The Soviet climb-down over Iran was confirmation that with Russia strength worked. As we have seen his Fulton thesis was vindicated. Violet Bonham Carter wrote to him, 'Events have powerfully reinforced your words.'[1]

The reception awaiting him in England was less confirmatory. Attlee had distanced himself from any overt criticism of Fulton and privately had expressed his 'warm thanks and appreciation' for Churchill's efforts on the loan.

The real push back was coming from Anthony Eden and Lord Salisbury of the Conservative Party in the House of Commons. On the very day that Churchill delivered his speech at Fulton, Eden was faced with a question from the Labour benches asking whether Churchill was about to make 'a sensational speech in America' putting Russia 'on the spot'.[2] Eden replied that he 'had not heard anything of the kind from my Right Honourable friend [Churchill] and I do not believe it for one single moment'.[3] Lord Salisbury, as David Reynolds writes in his insightful book *In Command of History*, believed that Fulton had 'strengthened the case for Churchill retiring from the Tory leadership'. If he did so 'he could say what he liked, without associating the Party with it' – an outcome devoutly to be wished for in Salisbury's view. As for Eden, wracked by his desire for a vacancy at Number 10, he hoped that Churchill would 'now be less anxious to lead' and would wish 'to pursue an anti-Russian crusade, independent of us'.

These views were to be aired at a dinner party with Eden scheduled for 9pm on the day of Churchill's arrival back in the

UK. Unfortunately the *Queen Mary* was delayed for several hours by fog in the Channel and it was 7pm before the liner had docked and Churchill could descend. Asked at the immediate press conference how he felt about parliamentary opinion, he quipped that he did not know the state of business in the House but 'I expect Mr Eden will tell me tonight'.[4]

We do not know what Eden said to Churchill at the long delayed dinner party but it would have been instantly obvious that Churchill's will to stay on had been massively reinforced by his US trip. This was not what Eden had expected or what he had hoped for. Churchill of course reported on his American trip to King George VI. On 12 March 1946, the king recorded his admiration for what Churchill had achieved: 'the whole world has been waiting for a statesman – and a statesman-like statement'. A month later the king dismissed Stalin's tirade against Churchill in his interview with *Pravda* saying that it merely 'showed he had a guilty conscience'. It is perhaps the clearest compliment. After all, the king had favoured Halifax's appointment over Churchill's in 1940.[5]

From the moment Churchill appeared on the bridge of the *Queen Mary* at Southampton, alongside his wife and Captain Ford, it was visually evident that he was back in form. Dressed in the uniform of an Elder Brother of Trinity House – one of his favourites – he doffed his cap and waved to the crowd who cheered enthusiastically. In New York, before he had left, he had stated unequivocally that he had 'no intention whatsoever of ceasing to lead the Conservative Party' and now his whole demeanour would prove it.[6] As David Reynolds comments, 'Buoyed up by his new celebrity status Churchill had hardened his mind against political retirement.'

Thus his American journey had ended. It had been dramatic and unprecedented – a defeated prime minister seeking to lead the world's most powerful nation to a new course, reversing Roosevelt's appeasement of Stalin, replacing, as Kennan would have seen it, optimism with realism. He had challenged and defied Stalin, seeking to unmask him as the tyrant he was – the marauder to be resisted. For this he needed maximum publicity and controversy; he had to fulfil his hope that 'over there' they would listen to him. And they had done so.

However, as we have seen, Churchill's message was more than that contained in his Fulton speech. His agenda was bolder and more comprehensive. His priority was to alert the USA to the Soviet threat and Fulton did that. But for his wake-up call to work, policies had to change and further policies brought forward. At Fulton he indicated the next imperative. His words were carefully chosen, as we have seen multiple times: 'The safety of the world requires a new unity in Europe, from which *no* nation should be permanently outcast.'

The policy he would call for next would be an almost unthinkable partnership between the pariah of Europe – Germany – and its implacable foe, France. Churchill's business for 1946 was thus far from over. After Fulton the platform would be Zurich. He had certainly determined not to retire from politics and his political activities would not be limited to Westminster. His agenda was to inspire a new Western alliance and a rejuvenated Europe was essential if the USA was to commit to its construction. It is the relationship between the Fulton speech and the one he was now about to deliver in Zurich that reveals his brilliance in that bleak year of 1946. The connection that he was to fashion illuminated world politics at the decisive moment forcing people to see their problems in a new light.

The sheer originality and force of what he intended he expressed exactly in an article he wrote for the *Daily Telegraph* at the close of the year. Europe's predicament, as he saw it, was in some ways even clearer than it had been immediately before the war. In that war the European peoples tore

> each other to pieces with more ferocity on a larger scale and with more deadly weapons than ever before. But have they found stable and lasting peace? Is the brotherhood of mankind any nearer? Has the Reign of Law returned? Alas, although the resources and vitality of nearly all the European countries are woefully diminished many of their old hatreds burn on with an undying flame.[7]

Churchill then conjures up an extraordinary image. He asks 'is there ever going to be an end?' He answers his own question:

> There is an old story of the Spanish prisoner pining for years in his dungeon and planning to escape. One day he pushes the door. It is open. It has always been open. He walks out free. Something like this opportunity lies before the peoples of Europe today.

Churchill had seen something no one else had seen. His vision stemmed from cardinal aspects of his character – his experience of dark depression, his courage, his compassion, and his extraordinary grasp of history and how apparent reality can be transformed if the motors of change are understood. He concluded his article 'the only worthwhile prize of Victory is the power to forgive and to guide and this is the price which glitters and shines beyond the French people'. It was the prize he offered them at Zurich.

In this speech he challenged the French to overcome their hatred of the Germans. His profound grasp of political realities was what ensured that this speech was not an overture in wishful thinking. Its bedrock was his insight into the motivation of his second country, the United States, and his sense of urgency because of the Soviet threat. Herein lies the link between these two speeches which together aimed to save the world. At Fulton he was confident that he could initiate the process of committing the USA to the defence of Western Europe. This was possible because of America's temporary monopoly of the atomic bomb. But Western Europe had to be revived economically, psychologically, spiritually. This could only happen with the reconciliation of France and Germany, impossible though that seemed. And why was this so essential? Because without it the USA would never pour its treasure into Europe's recovery. He understood the pre-condition of US generosity.

He also understood what he was up against. The French showed an almost Russian desire for revenge based on fear. They wanted reparations to cripple Germany and prevent any chance of it ever threatening France again. They demanded a permanent Allied occupation of the Ruhr – one in which, of course, the Soviet Union would have been delighted to participate. Britain and America saw this as a route to catastrophe. There could be no European recovery and no chance ultimately of safeguarding democracy in Western Europe without a healthy and vigorous West German economy. The French were bitterly opposed as de Gaulle was to make clear after the Zurich speech.

However, Churchill knew something else. George C. Marshall had been recalled by President Truman from his negotiations in China and it seemed clear that his focus would now be Europe and the Atlantic Alliance. He also knew from Marshall's opposition to Soviet proposals that the United States was moving to its own initiative on the restoration of the shattered economies of Europe. He was aware that there were powerful minds in Congress who questioned the brutal ending on Land-Lease to Britain and France. But to move American political opinion towards the grand ambition of what became the Marshall Plan would require a change of vision by the French. He could not have foreseen how events would conjoin to break through the impasse. He could not know as he approached his Zurich speech in September 1946 that Jean Monnet would persuade de Gaulle that without this plan for France's economic modernisation, France could never recover her greatness. Nor could he foresee that in Monnet's economic plan for France, George C. Marshall would recognise the outline of a 'much larger scale' programme 'involving several countries'.[8] Nor could he foresee that Monnet and France's foreign minister, Robert Schuman, would succeed within a year in persuading the French government to propose a merger of the coal and steel industries of Germany and France, thus meeting America's demand for a quite revolutionary level of European co-operation. Churchill could not have predicted this remarkable sequence of changing interests and perceptions. Neither could he have known that Marshall's plan would save Monnet's plan and this would mitigate de Gaulle's initial rejection of all he would say at Zurich. But what Churchill's instinct told him on the eve of Zurich was enough. He knew that once again he could grasp the mantle of history and, by doing so, demonstrate that democracies did not need to be imprisoned by the past. Like the Spanish prisoner they could find the dungeon door open.

In his Zurich speech, Churchill led the prisoner to the dungeon door he imagined locked for ever and urged him to push it open: France – defeated, occupied, liberated. France, exhausted and

embittered, could 'exercise the only worthwhile prize of Victory
... the power to forgive'. In understanding this potential for transformation and initiating the process through his words, Churchill
demonstrated the power of his maxim 'In Victory, Magnanimity'.

So it is now to Churchill's Zurich speech that we must turn and
to the extraordinary reversal of US policy towards Europe insti-
gated by the arrival of George C. Marshall as the US secretary of
state. Churchill's two 1946 speeches – Fulton and Zurich – constitute a vital prelude to America's change of heart, and of mind.

PART V

EUROPE RESTORED

16

Zurich

'I am now going to say something that will astonish you . . .'

As with his Fulton speech, Churchill's second great intervention of 1946 was activated by an academic invitation facilitated by a holiday. There was a conjunction of platform, pleasure and the hinge of fate. To put it another way, Churchill believed in seizing the hem of history and in September 1946 he did not doubt he held it in his grip. He was not the dispirited man who in the previous year had spotted the opportunity provided by Truman's footnote on the invitation from Westminster College in Missouri. He was newly invigorated and confident. Thus the invitation now before him, to speak at the University of Zurich, represented an opportunity he grasped without hesitation. It was made all the more attractive by the Swiss government's offer of an excellent holiday in their country, as their guest.

In August, accompanied by his wife, Clementine, and his daughter, Mary, he arrived in Switzerland to savour Swiss hospitality. Churchill rejoiced in its undamaged beauty, an oasis at the heart of war-torn Europe, and received endless tributes to his statesmanship and Britain's wartime courage. He returned the flattery with his own. On arriving in Zurich at the Town Hall, showered with flowers and the cheers of the crowd, he said to the Swiss:

> You have solved many of the difficulties which have led other countries into suffering and misfortune. You have thus managed to be united in spite of the differences of language and race and there is no reason why your example should not be followed throughout the whole of this wrecked continent of Europe.[1]

His purpose was not to advocate the neutrality that had kept Switzerland out of the war. The last thing he wanted was a neutral Western Europe, helpless before Stalin. His wish, fervently held, was for Western Europe to unite, economically, politically, spiritually – overcoming the 'differences of language and race'. The idea of a restored Europe would motivate and justify the commitment of the USA. It would be helped by Britain and the Commonwealth. It could turn the tide in what would soon be recognised as the Cold War.

For this to happen, however, Churchill would once again, as at Fulton, have to startle and indeed 'astonish' the world. He knew he had the power to provoke and inspire and, since Fulton, he also knew that he had the authority to do so. This time was different in that he did not need the backing of the British Foreign Office, which he neither requested nor received. This was *his* moment and he would fulfil his mission by articulating a vision of European reconciliation so bold that Europe's self-awareness would be reshaped for ever.

To the crowds around the Town Hall, who cheered him to the echo every time he waved his famous 'V for Victory' hand-sign, Churchill paused to explain that this, his most defiant and famous gesture, now had a different meaning. It no longer 'stood for the victory of one group of nations over another, but for the victory of personal liberty over tyranny everywhere'.[2]

In a single sentence and a simple gesture, he had spelt out his leitmotiv with the commanding clarity that occurs at productions of Wagner in Bayreuth. There a trumpet plays the leitmotiv of the opera before the audience enters the theatre. With his gesture and single sentence before his speech at Zurich, Churchill had sounded the note he needed and set the tone for what was to follow. The 'V' sign was no longer about defiance but about reconciliation.

In victory, there needed to be more than magnanimity. There had to be, in the words of Gladstone, which he would borrow in his speech, 'a blessed act of oblivion'. His call would be for 'an end to retribution'. There was, in Churchill the warrior, a dimension of forgiveness and the realism of a statesman who understood that without forgiveness reconciliation would be impossible and that without reconciliation no restoration of Europe would be feasible.

This perception was at the heart of what he was about to say to his audience in the Great Hall at Zurich University.

Inside the hall was an audience somewhat smaller than that in Fulton but no less attentive. As at Fulton, there was also a global audience for media interest and the speech would be broadcast. Again, as at Fulton, there was academic formality. He was welcomed by the rector who was effusive in his praise of Churchill and of Britain, presenting him with an illuminated address of thanks. The rostrum was decked with flowers, the banners of all the student corporations were displayed. The scene was set.

The speech itself is laid out in full below, but before the text, it is important to identify its highlights and explain its structure. In the following chapter I will describe the reactions to the speech, especially those in Britain and France.

The speech challenged the status quo as robustly as Fulton, and the response was just as divided. Churchill's oratorical skill at Zurich matches that of Fulton, but the speech was shorter, less embellished and less Victorian, yet it depicts danger as graphically and advocates a response with greater simplicity and directness. In writing his Fulton speech, Churchill had grappled with a surfeit of themes – the two great 'marauders' menacing free men, namely war and tyranny; the affinity of values and language binding together Britain, the Commonwealth and the USA in an alliance that had to be made militarily effective; and the reality of the Iron Curtain.

At Zurich he focused exclusively on a message he presaged at Fulton – 'the awful ruin of Europe', 'a new unity' in Europe needed for the 'safety of the world', and how to initiate its creation. In both speeches the atomic bomb is both a window of opportunity and the harbinger of doom.

The power of the speech is its moral insight and the realism of its reading of relevant history. Its boldness lies in its call for Franco-German partnership – an idea made more shocking, even repugnant, by the daily revelations of German atrocities and war crimes emerging from the Nuremberg trials then under way. It pays tribute to the idealism of Count Coudenhove-Kalergi and Astride Briand and their advocacy of a 'kind of United States of Europe' – a phrase that he uses while remaining clear about Britain's relationship with their initiative. In examining the reactions to the speech, we will return to the impact of the Nuremberg trials and the seeds of ambiguity sown on Britain's view of what eventually emerged in the Treaty of Rome as 'ever closer Union'.

But for now, let us turn to the actual text of Churchill's second seminal speech of 1946.

'Europe Arise' Zurich, 19 September 1946, by Winston Churchill[3]

I wish to speak to you today about the tragedy of Europe. This noble continent, comprising on the whole the fairest and the most cultivated regions of the earth; enjoying a temperate and equable climate, is the home of all the great parent races of the western world. It is the fountain of Christian faith and Christian ethics. It is the origin of most of the culture, arts, philosophy and science both of ancient and modern times. If Europe were once united in the sharing of its common inheritance, there would be no limit to the happiness, to the prosperity and glory which its three or four hundred million people would enjoy. Yet it is from Europe that have sprung that series of frightful nationalistic quarrels, originated by the Teutonic nations, which we have seen even in this twentieth century and in our own lifetime, wreck the peace and mar the prospects of all mankind.

And what is the plight to which Europe has been reduced? Some of the smaller States have indeed made a good recovery, but over wide areas a vast quivering mass of tormented, hungry, careworn and bewildered human beings gape at the ruins of their cities and homes, and scan the dark horizons for the approach of some new peril, tyranny or terror. Among the victors there is a babel of jarring voices; among the vanquished the sullen silence of despair. That is all that Europeans, grouped in so many ancient States and nations, that is all that the Germanic Powers have got by tearing each other to pieces and spreading havoc far and wide. Indeed, but for the fact that the great Republic across the Atlantic Ocean has at length realised that the ruin or enslavement of Europe would involve their own fate as well, and has stretched out hands of succour and guidance, the Dark Ages would have returned in all their cruelty and squalor. They may still return.

Yet all the while there is a remedy which, if it were generally and spontaneously adopted, would as if by a miracle transform the whole scene, and would in a few years make all Europe, or the greater part of it, as free and as happy as Switzerland is today. What is this sovereign remedy? It is to re-create the European Family, or as much of it as we can, and provide it with a structure under which it can dwell in peace, in safety and in freedom. We must build a kind of United States of Europe. In this way only will hundreds of millions of toilers be able to regain the simple joys and hopes which make life worth living. The process is simple. All that is needed is the resolve of hundreds of millions of men and women to do right instead of wrong, and gain as their reward, blessing instead of cursing.

Much work has been done upon this task by the exertions of the Pan-European Union which owes so much to Count Coudenhove-Kalergi and which commanded the services of the famous French patriot and statesman Aristide Briand. There is also that immense body of doctrine and procedure, which was brought into being amid high hopes after the First World War, as the League of Nations. The League of Nations did not fail because of its principles or conceptions. It failed because these principles were deserted by those States who had brought it into being. It failed because the Governments of those days feared to face the facts and act while time remained. This disaster must not be repeated. There is, therefore, much knowledge and material with which to build; and also bitter dear-bought experience. I was very glad to read in the newspapers two days ago that my friend President Truman had expressed his interest and sympathy with this great design. There is no reason why a regional organisation of Europe should in any way conflict with the world organisation of the United Nations. On the contrary, I believe that the larger synthesis will only survive if it is founded upon coherent natural groupings. There is already a natural grouping in the Western Hemisphere. We British have our own Commonwealth of Nations. These do not weaken, on the contrary they strengthen, the world organisation. They are in fact its main support.

And why should there not be a European group which could give a sense of enlarged patriotism and common citizenship to the distracted peoples of this turbulent and mighty continent and why should it not take its rightful place with other great groupings in shaping the destinies of men?

In order that this should be accomplished, there must be an act of faith in which millions of families speaking many languages must consciously take part.

We all know that the two world wars through which we have passed arose out of the vain passion of a newly united Germany to play the dominating part in the world. In this last struggle crimes and massacres have been committed for which there is no parallel since the invasions of the Mongols in the fourteenth century and no equal at any time in human history. The guilty must be punished. Germany must be deprived of the power to rearm and make another aggressive war.

But when all this has been done, as it will be done, as it is being done, there must be an end to retribution. There must be what Mr Gladstone many years ago called 'a blessed act of oblivion'.

We must all turn our backs upon the horrors of the past. We must look to the future. We cannot afford to drag forward across the years that are to come the hatreds and revenges which have sprung from the injuries of the past. If Europe is to be saved from infinite misery, and indeed from final doom, there must be an act of faith in the European family and an act of oblivion against all the crimes and follies of the past.

Can the free peoples of Europe rise to the height of these resolves of the soul and instincts of the spirit of man? If they can, the wrongs and injuries which have been inflicted will have been washed away on all sides by the miseries which have been endured. Is there any need for further floods of agony? Is it the only lesson of history that mankind is unteachable? Let there be justice, mercy and freedom. The peoples have only to will it, and all will achieve their hearts' desire.

I am now going to say something that will astonish you. The first step in the re-creation of the European family must be a partnership between France and Germany. In this way only can France recover the moral leadership of Europe. There can be no revival of Europe without a spiritually great France and a spiritually great Germany. The structure of the United States of Europe, if well and truly built, will be such as to make the material strength of a single state less important. Small nations will count as much as large ones and gain their honour by their contribution to the common cause. The ancient states and principalities of Germany, freely joined together for mutual convenience in a federal system, might each take their individual place among the United States of Europe. I shall not try to make a detailed programme for hundreds of millions of people who want to be happy and free, prosperous and safe, who wish to enjoy the four freedoms of which the great President Roosevelt spoke, and live in accordance with the principles embodied in the Atlantic Charter. If this is their wish, they have only to say so, and means can certainly be found, and machinery erected, to carry that wish into full fruition.

But I must give you warning. Time may be short. At present there is a breathing-space. The cannon have ceased firing. The fighting has stopped; but the dangers have not stopped.

If we are to form the United States of Europe or whatever name or form it may take, we must begin now.

In these present days we dwell strangely and precariously under the shield and protection of the atomic bomb. The atomic bomb is still only in the hands of a State and nation which we know will never use it except in the cause of right and freedom. But it may well be that in a few years this awful agency of destruction will be widespread and the catastrophe following from its use by several warring nations will not only bring to an end all that we call civilisation, but may possibly disintegrate the globe itself.

I must now sum up the propositions which are before you. Our constant aim must be to build and fortify the strength of the United Nations Organisation. Under and within that world concept, we must re-create the European family in a regional structure called, it may be, the United States of Europe. The first step is to form a Council of Europe. If at first all the States of Europe are not willing or able to join the Union, we must nevertheless proceed to assemble and combine those who will and those who can. The salvation of the common people of every race and of every land from war or servitude must be established on solid foundations and must be guarded by the readiness of all men and women to die rather than submit to tyranny. In all this urgent work, France and Germany must take the lead together. Great Britain, the British Commonwealth of Nations, mighty America, and I trust Soviet Russia – for then indeed all would be well – must be the friends and sponsors of the new Europe and must champion its right to live and shine. Therefore I say to you: let Europe arise!

This then was a speech that was careful to stress the compatibility of what he was proposing with other features of the emerging and established international order. It did not threaten the world organisation of the United Nations. It was important to emphasise this given Roosevelt's urgent advocacy of the UN, which overrode all his other concerns during his last conversations with Stalin. Churchill had, as ever, a close eye on US public opinion. He had shocked many Americans by what he had said at Fulton, a negative reaction influenced, and to an extent, led by, the Roosevelt family.

For the same reason he stressed specifically that he was 'very glad' that two days earlier his 'friend President Truman had expressed his interest with this great project'.

Nor did his call for European unity, based on the reconciliation of France and Germany and indeed *led* by them, conflict with Britain's unique alliance with the USA and its ties with the Empire and Commonwealth. Indeed, all was not only compatible but interrelated, even interdependent. Yet no matter how emollient Churchill wished to sound, there was no disguising and no wish to disguise the salient features of the speech that determined the reactions to it both then and since then.

He had proposed that Germany be re-admitted to the family of the European nations despite all the German atrocities and crimes being reported afresh every day. He had proposed that all the hatred engendered by the barbarous behaviour of the Nazis be consigned to 'oblivion' once the conspicuously guilty on trial at Nuremberg and elsewhere had been punished. He had proposed a 'kind of United States of Europe' but not that Britain should be a member of it. Britain's posture would be supportive, not participatory.

Above all else he clearly did not see Russia or its satellite states as members. He was urging an alliance capable of containing Soviet ambition.

Churchill's vision was shaped by two of his most powerful intellectual and emotional instincts. Having witnessed the utter devastation of Berlin in 1945, he confessed that his hatred of the Germans had died within him. But he also knew that the European tragedy had happened because the democracies, including the USA, had appeased evil. His Zurich speech was born of his own emotional accommodation with Germany and the Germans after their defeat, and his intellectual determination to ensure that tyranny not be appeased a second time.

17

Reactions II

Reactions to Churchill's Zurich speech were both immediate and long lasting. One of the first, however, proved less enduring than others. It was the fear that his words were, as *The Times* put it the next day, based 'on the assumption that Europe is already irrevocably divided between East and West'. In its editorial opinion it saw this as 'the peril of his argument and of its enunciation at this moment'.[1]

This concern was exacerbated by the conviction that Churchill must be speaking on behalf of the British government although, as we have already seen, he neither requested not received any endorsement from either the Foreign Office or Number 10. The *Manchester Guardian*'s diplomatic correspondent writing from Paris was disapproving:

> Great importance is attached here to the speech of the British Opposition Leader. Far too many people seriously believe that the Opposition Leader is expressing the views held by the Government, but which for diplomatic reasons, members of the Cabinet are unwilling to express . . . it seems unfortunate that Mr. Churchill did not take this common misconception into account in drafting his Zurich speech.[2]

In an echo of Lord Halifax's dismay after the Fulton speech – that Stalin would be so offended that any hope of maintaining or reviving the wartime alliance would be lost – some commentators deplored its likely effect. The *Manchester Guardian* was particularly distressed. It wrote: 'It would seem impossible to convince representatives to the Eastern bloc that members of the opposition [Churchill] play any other function than that of mouthpieces of "British Imperial Policy"!'[3]

Churchill's Zurich speech coincided with a series of international conferences attempting to keep the diplomatic interchange of the wartime alliance alive. The last of these was to occur in 1947 in Moscow, attended for the first time by America's new secretary of state, George C. Marshall. It would set the seal on the rejection by both him and Britain's foreign secretary, Ernest Bevin, of Moscow's intransigence over Germany. But Churchill's initiative in September 1946 was the first clear call for a united Western response to Stalin based on the return of Germany to the European family. To Western commentators committed to the purity of the wartime alliance between the West and the USSR, this was anathema and they declared it so. Ironically they were right in one regard. Churchill was indeed, at that time, only speaking for himself.

Thus this editorial in Britain's *Reynolds News* on 22 September 1946, entitled 'Churchillism':[4]

Mr. Churchill, in his Fulton speech, called for an Anglo-American alliance. In his speech at Zurich on Thursday he called for a new European alliance, headed by France and Germany, under the sponsorship of the Anglo-American alliance, and with the atomic bomb as its 'shield and protection'.

Mr. Churchill does not say so in so many words, but the whole tenor of his Fulton and Zurich speeches makes it clear that he wants this fabric of alliances as a means of isolating the Soviet Union. Between Russia and the West there are many differences still to be settled and a dismal chapter of mutual irritations to be forgotten. Mr. Churchill's plan will do neither. His persistent peddling of the idea of an American–West European Power Bloc can only deepen Soviet suspicions and make more difficult the task of reconciliation.

The British Government should make it clear that when Mr. Churchill hawks around his new version of the *cordon sanitaire* he is speaking for himself – and nobody else.

The reason the rejection of Churchill's approach so trenchantly explained above did not last long was that it was overtaken by events. Stalin's obduracy and Molotov's negativity proved beyond doubt to Britain and the USA at governmental level by 1947 that there was no deal available with Moscow on the future of Germany and that the reconstruction of Western Europe was the unavoidable imperative.

Far more problematic, in September 1946, was the French reaction. *The Times* raised the right questions after Churchill's Zurich speech. It stated that while the speech demonstrated his 'familiar characteristics . . . of courage and imagination', it prescribed a remedy 'which Europe, in its present condition, showed few signs of accepting'. Why? Its reasoning was clear: 'Germany today is in no position to offer partnership to anyone' and 'it remains to be seen whether French opinion will be prepared to tolerate, even from Mr. Churchill, the suggestion that the first step in the recreation of the European family must be a partnership between France and Germany'. Indeed Churchill's speech 'dumbfounded French opinion' in the judgement of both politicians and the press.[5] Indeed as Churchill had predicted, the French were astonished but, more than that, they were appalled.

A powerful reason for this was the confirmation from the trials at Nuremberg and from many other emerging sources of just how horrendous the atrocities perpetrated by the Third Reich had been, including those committed on French soil.

The French had recently executed Pierre Laval, the former foreign minister who had collaborated with the Nazis after the German occupation. He was shot on 15 October 1945. The International Military Tribunal set up by the four wartime allies, by then including France, met the same month. There was no precedent for what they decided. They would put on trial the leaders of the Third Reich whom they had in custody including Goering, Ribbentrop, Keitel, Streicher and Speer, among others. The trial was held in one of the few large buildings still standing in what had been Hitler's showpiece city for the Nazi movement – Nuremberg. It was an appropriate location as Nuremberg had hosted vast Nazi rallies. Had Hitler won the war it would have been turned into a marble and granite complex of buildings glorifying the Führer and his intended 1000-year Reich. Work had started before the war using Jewish prisoners from nearby concentration camps. Nuremberg had also been the place where the anti-Semitic legislation known as the Nuremberg Laws had been proclaimed – formalising the legal framework which would lead to the mass murder of the Jews, first deprived of all rights, and then of life itself.

Prominent Nazis who had not already committed suicide like Hitler, Himmler and Goebbels, or who had not disappeared like Bormann, faced four indictments summarised by the pre-eminent historian of the Holocaust, Martin Gilbert. First, 'a common plan or conspiracy to seize power and establish a totalitarian regime to prepare and wage a war of aggression'; second 'waging a war of aggression'; third, 'Violation of the laws of war'; and fourth, 'Crimes against humanity, persecution, and extermination'.[6]

The charges were not only unprecedented, they were also controversial. The notorious president of the German Red Cross, the chief surgeon to the SS, shouted on the scaffold, 'This is nothing but political revenge!'[7] He fully deserved his death but of the four indictments only the fourth escaped any criticism. Even Churchill remarked to General Ismay at the time, 'you and I must take care not to lose the next war', an observation described wryly by A. J. P. Taylor as 'a wise verdict on the proceedings at Nuremberg'.

It was their crimes against humanity, including extermination, that utterly revolted the world and turned Germany into a pariah nation. Yet it was this shamed and shameful people that Churchill now proposed should join with France. To the French, shamed by their capitulation and occupation, the concept was profoundly shocking and must have seemed extremely hazardous. Their wish was that Germany remain excluded and occupied in its turn. Their fear was that Germany was inherently stronger than France, larger by population, and once economically recovered, far more powerful.

As we have seen, France, in part, mirrored the Soviet attitude towards Germany. Both feared Germany and both were determined to prevent any restoration of its economic power. No one expressed this view more trenchantly than General de Gaulle. After Churchill had delivered his Zurich speech he penned a letter to de Gaulle seeking to explain why he believed France and Germany had to become reconciled. He entrusted the letter to Duncan Sandys, his son-in-law, who took it to his home in

Colombey. What transpired must have been extremely upsetting to Sandys. Indeed, he went on to found the European Movement and to play a leading role in advocating the cause. What de Gaulle had to say to him at Colombey was the opposite of what he wished to hear. Martin Gilbert and others have recorded Sandys' account. The General said:

> that the reference in Mr. Churchill's Zurich speech to a Franco-German partnership had been badly received in France. Germany as a state no longer existed. The French were violently opposed to recreating any kind of unified, centralised Reich and were gravely suspicious of the policy of the American and British governments.

If this was not clear enough, de Gaulle shared his deadliest fears. He believed that 'unless steps were taken to reinvent the resuscitation of German power, there was the danger that a United Europe would become nothing else than an enlarged Germany'. General de Gaulle's solution was brutal – the permanent allocation to France of all coal produced by the Ruhr, the long-term occupation by French forces of North Rhineland, which should be at once incorporated into France's Zone of Occupation, and the establishment of international control of all the industries of the Ruhr under certain conditions to be agreed by France. In conclusion, de Gaulle threw open his arms, saying 'Voilà, mes conditions!'[8]

How was this French attitude changed? The impact of US aid to all Western Europe under the aegis of the Marshall Plan transformed the economic situation in both France and Germany. And at the heart of that strategy of transformation would lie the unique contribution of the remarkable French.

In 1946, Jean Monnet[9] was little known to the public in France, Britain or Germany. But he was known to the architects of the emerging Atlantic Alliance – to Churchill with whom he had drawn up plans for a union of France and the UK in the terrible weeks in 1940 before the French surrender made them redundant. Of Churchill, he believed that he was a man with the courage and imagination to create new worlds. In his view, the French owed him an immense debt.

Monnet was also known to de Gaulle for whom he worked in wartime London. After the Liberation, de Gaulle turned to Monnet to develop and implement 'Le Plan', the programme of investment and direction that began by early 1947 to modernise the French economy. 'I told de Gaulle,' he said, 'you speak of French strength, of French power, but we have none until our economy is rebuilt as one that is modern and competitive.'

To achieve this, Monnet would depend critically on the other people who knew him well, the power brokers in the USA. Monnet had worked in New York and Washington between the wars, winning the attention of both Roosevelt and George C. Marshall. Of the Americans, Monnet was impressed by 'their energy, their instinct for a solution, and their optimism'. But the quality he most admired was 'their generosity . . . whatever people may say, they did not enter the war for themselves. They did it because of their commitment to liberty.'

It was, of course, ultimately their commitment to liberty that drove their resistance to the threat posed by Soviet ambition. It was to that commitment to freedom that Churchill appealed at Fulton and again at Zurich. It is central to the Truman Doctrine enunciated in 1947 and the Marshall Plan's motivation, both described in the next chapter.

It was Monnet along with the foreign minister of France, Robert Schuman, who would together realise Churchill's vision of Franco-German leadership by proposing and successfully negotiating the European Coal and Steel Community, linking the industries of both countries and transforming 'the sinews of war into the bonds of peace'.[10]

There remains the longest-lasting reaction to the ideas proposed by Churchill in Zurich – the reaction of the British. Nothing was to compare to the protracted, bitter political division that had dominated so much of Britain's debate with itself and with others ever since Zurich.

In the Zurich speech, Churchill had acknowledged the earlier influence of a quixotic and formidable personality, Count Coudenhove-Kalergi. Churchill had renewed contact with the Count shortly before his Zurich speech and with the former French prime minister, Leon Blum, after the speech. At Zurich he claimed that he had 'revived the ancient and glorious conception of a United Europe associated before the war with the names of M. Briand and Count Coudenhove-Kalergi which I had supported for many years'.[11] In this correspondence, published in their study of 'British Engagement with the Pan-European Ideal 1929–48', the historians Richard Carr and Bradley Hart reveal how from the moment of Churchill's public endorsement of European union, he would find himself immersed in divisive argument. Blum's criticism was that by championing the idea, Churchill would give the idea of European federalism 'a character too narrowly Churchillian', which would result in 'the embarrassment, circumspection, and hesitation of the Labour Party and, in consequence, of international Socialism'. Churchill retorted that his support for this idea was absolutely not partisan in any political party sense.

The idea of European federalism had become a party political football in British politics, with the reoccurring pattern of British parties being sympathetic to European Union while in opposition, and hostile when in government. The reality is that even British Conservatives who recognised the imperative of European Union if future wars were to be avoided remained ambiguous about British involvement. Long before Churchill's own reticence about the nature of British participation as opposed to membership, one of the first Tories approached by Coudenhove-Kalergi in the late 1920s rebutted him. Leo Amery wrote to him that the British 'were much too far from Europe ever to enter wholeheartedly into its policies'.

I had the opportunity to examine this British reluctance with two key figures in the relationship. One was Duncan Sandys who, as we have seen, was sent to Colombey les deux Eglises to try to persuade de Gaulle to soften his attack on Churchill's Zurich speech. Later Sandys founded the European Movement. He reminded me that as Britain emerged from the war, largely bankrupt but as a victorious power, its view of European Union would always be different from those defeated and occupied in the war, meaning France and Germany. Jean Monnet admitted to me that he had never tried too hard to persuade the British to join the Coal and Steel Community. Nor was he too dismayed by the UK's refusal to engage in the Messina Conference which led to the establishment of the Common Market. He knew that it was not 'natural' for nations to unite and that they would only do so when such a step became inevitable. That moment did arrive, for Harold Macmillan and Harold Wilson, and subsequently Edward Heath sealed the deal with the French. On the way to that moment in 1973 and ever since, Churchill has been hijacked by Europhiles and Europhobes. For the latter, Churchill epitomises defiance of

Europe. For Europhiles, he was the enthusiastic advocate of European union.

So he was, but critically he never advocated British membership. He had not succeeded in saving the Empire but he had saved a global role for Britain. It was based on the alliance with the USA, on the British Commonwealth, and it desperately needed a restored Europe. His two 1946 speeches addressed these themes – acting as a clarion call only just in time to enable the West to counter the Soviet threat.

Returning to London by plane with his wife and daughter, Churchill already knew that his speech at Zurich University would have profound influence. The short flight to Hendon did not match the excitement of his journey back to Washington in the president's train after his speech at Westminster College in Fulton, Missouri. On the flight there was no non-family member to whom he could declare, as he had on returning from Fulton, that this was 'the most important' speech of his life. Yet he deserved to feel that it was undoubtedly the second most important speech he had given in that critical year of 1946. In little more than six months, he had changed perceptions and altered the horizons of the West.

Paradoxically, while US assertiveness in what was becoming the Cold War was what Churchill had wanted, its pace and extent also increasingly concerned him. Churchill's purpose was not only to stop Stalin – it was to force him to negotiate. He wanted dialogue. He believed in summitry. As he made clear, he saw the objective of Western rearmament not as war but as its avoidance once the Soviets had been forced to recognise the resolve and recovery of the West.

As we turn to America's change of position, it will be necessary to recognise it was not entirely to Churchill's taste. What mattered in the two years after Zurich was the mighty achievements of US policy – reversing the unreality and appeasement of Roosevelt's approach to Stalin. In 1946 Churchill called for two things above all else – that the USA with Britain demonstrate the political will and military capability to deter Stalin, and that the economic recovery of Europe proceed as fast as possible powered by American aid and facilitated by growing European co-operation. By the end of 1949 Stalin's grab for Berlin had been thwarted, the Marshall Plan was under way, the Federal Republic of Germany had been established and NATO was being set up. It was a breath-taking advance wresting the initiative from the Kremlin.

Those who played a part in it recognised its scale and stature. They were 'present at the Creation' and Churchill had been the first to arrive.

The USA: From Irritation to Determination

At root, Churchill was always optimistic about the USA. Half-American through his mother, his instinct was to view any cup offered by the USA as half-full not half-empty. It was this tendency that led him into his parliamentary folly over the terms of the loan to Britain proposed by Washington in 1945. Yet equally it was this optimism that had kept him going during the darkest days of the war. The Americans had agreed Lend-Lease in 1941 but it was far too little to turn the tide of war. That spring, Churchill had been forced to evacuate British forces for the second time – from Crete not France – and Joe Kennedy, when US ambassador in London, had been pessimistic about Britain's chances. There seemed no likelihood of America joining the war. However, on 27 April, he went on air quoting Arthur Hugh Clough's poem:

> For while the tired waves, vainly breaking
> Seem here no painful inch to gain
> Far back through creeks and inlets waking
> Comes silent, flooding in, the main.
>
> And not by Eastern windows only
> When daylight comes, comes in the light:

In front the sun climbs slow, how slowly.
But Westward, look, the land is bright.[1]

That was how Churchill saw it in 1941. It was how he saw it also in 1946.

He was sure that his message at Fulton would galvanise Americans whether they at first agreed with it or not. The assessment by the British Foreign Office on Fulton and its impact confirmed this. It found that while many, especially in the US military, supported what Churchill had said, it had also been condemned by many in Congress, the media and amongst the general public. It had also – as we have seen – been disowned by the Truman administration. But the FCO report concluded that the speech had given 'the sharpest jolt to American thinking of any utterance since the end of the war'. It would 'set the pattern of discussion on world affairs for some time to come'.[2]

Thus Churchill would not have been surprised by the turn of events and the stiffening of US resolve that emerged after his seminal speeches at Fulton and Zurich. This is not to argue that these speeches caused the events of America's increasingly public reaction and eventual pre-emption of them, but the FCO report's judgement can be applied to both Fulton and Zurich. They were indeed the catalyst for discussion in Europe and America.

Two sets of events ultimately forced the change from American irritation to US official determination. First was the character of Soviet conquest and occupation in Eastern and Central Europe. The second was Britain's inability to contain the Soviet threat given the parlous state of her economy coupled with the disarray and destruction in Western Europe. It was time for America to pick up and wear the mantle of leadership

that had to pass from Britain to the USA. Any return to isolationism would – as Churchill's speeches predicted – condemn
Europe to Soviet domination. As it was, matters had been left so
late that – as we will see – the US government had to contem-
plate and, at least in principle, agree to the possibility of
deploying its one sovereign advantage – the A-bomb – if Stalin
moved to take Germany.

Stalin's thinking was on the record. On 9 February in Moscow
he had beaten the drum. The war had been caused by the 'capi-
talist monopolies'. They were still there. Thus 'the USSR must
treble the basic materials of national defence'. George Kennan
had argued that the USSR was 'committed fanatically to the
belief that . . . there can be no permanent modus vivendi with
the US'. At the same time, Britain's foreign secretary, Ernest
Bevin, told his prime minister that 'the Russians have decided
on an aggressive policy based upon militant communism and
Russian chauvinism . . . and seem determined to stop at nothing
short of war'.[3]

The one – for the time being – unique factor in America's
favour was the A-bomb, but this could disappear. When Truman
had told Stalin at Potsdam of America's successful testing of 'a
new bomb of extraordinary power',[4] Stalin showed no surprise.
His spies embedded in the Manhattan Project had warned him
but also alerted him to the reality that 'as yet the Americans only
possessed one or two bombs'.[5] These they were to use over
Hiroshima and Nagasaki.

Stalin had Eastern and Central Europe in his grip. His control
of the Kremlin was total. Those in his immediate circle were terri-
fied of him. His paranoia was such that he trusted no one but
equally no one could trust him. His silences could threaten extinc-
tion or imprisonment for oneself or any member of one's family.

No one was safe. Of course he bribed as well as bullied. In Simon Sebag Montefiore's telling phrase,[6] corruption was

> the untold story of Stalin's post-war terror – the magnates and marshals plundered Europe with the avarice of Goering . . . Stalin's potentates now existed in a hot house of rarefied privilege bedecked with fine Persian carpets . . . their houses were palatial . . . the dachas of the Mikoyans, Molotovs and Voroshilovs were crammed with gifts from workers . . . rugs, gold Caucasian weapons, porcelain.

The richest pickings came from the countries the Red Army had liberated. Anne Applebaum, in her study of the Gulag, describes how 'all across Central Europe, the Soviet Union's great strength as an occupying power was its ability to corrupt local elites, to turn them into collaborators who willingly oppressed their own people'.[7]

Always behind the corruption was terror. Stalin had been frank to the Yugoslav Molovan Djilas and others when he enunciated his reality of conquest – 'whoever occupies a territory also imposes on it his own social system as far as his army can reach'. His army had reached Berlin and its military preponderance held the potential for far greater extension. Only the atomic bomb could balance Soviet strength and one way in which Stalin could destroy this advantage lay in the fact that, as Applebaum notes, 'Concentration camps were a fundamental part of the Soviet social system.' These now appeared across Soviet Europe and, as in the USSR itself, the slave labour they provided was essential to Russia's military-industrial complex. In Czechoslovakia, eighteen special camps were grouped around the uranium mines of Yachimov. The inmates mined the uranium for Stalin's atom bomb. They did so without any protective clothing and very many died.

Beria, Stalin's head of the Soviet police and, under 'the boss' himself, the man with the most power over the Gulag, was put in charge of creating the bomb. This project was to have overriding priority. Beria's spies within the Manhattan Project were invaluable. So too were German scientists captured at the war's end, as well as many brilliant Russian physicists – all isolated and guarded. But equally important was Stalin's denial of higher living standards for the Russians themselves, which released resources for the Soviet atomic bomb programme, including the ever available labour of the Soviet penal camps.

This bleak reality was partly known and partly guessed at by Western intelligence and Western leaders. Churchill was disingenuous in claiming that the West knew nothing of what was happening behind the Iron Curtain. But the most direct indication of Russia's obsessive urgency in marshalling and increasing its material resources focused on the demand for reparations from Germany. So strident did this become that it furnished America's new secretary of state, George C. Marshall, with his sticking point with the Russians during his first and last full conference with them in Moscow. It proved to be the final – the 43rd – conference of the wartime alliance of foreign ministers. It was held on 24 March 1947. The meeting itself was preceded by a screening of a new Soviet colour film based on a Russian folk story, 'The Snow Flower'. Stalin demanded that the USA and UK make good on what he claimed he had been promised by Roosevelt before his death – $10 billion of German reparations.

The scene had been set earlier by a glacial Molotov, making it clear that if Germany was allowed to fuse into one economic entity – the direction advocated by the West – then it could only happen if the UK and USA ensured this reparation. In practice that would have meant Britain and America subsidising their zones in order to make payments. The Soviet zone was already being stripped of its factories and economic assets with guarded trains leaving daily loaded with machine tools and factory parts destined for Russia. Bevin and Marshall had seen through this and challenged the Russian approach time and time again.

Now at this final meeting, Marshall and Bevin 'had had enough'.[8] Marshall expressed bluntly his frustration. Enough attempts had been made to negotiate with the Russians but 'I decided finally at Moscow after the War that they could not be negotiated with'.[9] On his flight back to Washington his translator later remembered that 'Stalin's seeming indifference to what was happening in Germany made a deep impression on Marshall'. The secretary of state saw how perilous was Europe's economic predicament: 'Millions of people were on short rations. There was a danger of epidemics ... this was the kind of crisis that Communism thrived on.'[10]

Marshall was now committed to a programme of US aid and reconstruction. It would become the Marshall Plan and it forms a key part of America's change of heart. The other key element had occurred just before Marshall's conference with the Russians in Moscow. It was President Truman's speech to Congress broadcast to the nation on 12 March 1947. In it, he enunciated what became known as the Truman Doctrine. The key passage was as follows:

> The peoples of a number of countries of the world have recently had totalitarian regimes forced upon them against their will. The Government of the United States has made frequent protests against coercion and intimidation, in violation of the Yalta agreement, in Poland, Rumania, and Bulgaria. I must also state that in a number of other countries there have been similar developments.

At the present moment in world history nearly every nation must choose between alternative ways of life. The choice is too often not a free one.

One way of life is based upon the will of the majority, and is distinguished by free institutions, representative government, free elections, guarantees of individual liberty, freedom of speech and religion, and freedom from political oppression.

The second way of life is based upon the will of a minority forcibly imposed upon the majority. It relies upon terror and oppression, a controlled press and radio; fixed elections, and the suppression of personal freedoms.

I believe that it must be the policy of the United States to support free peoples who are resisting attempted subjugation by armed minorities or by outside pressures.

I believe that we must assist free peoples to work out their own destinies in their own way.

I believe that our help should be primarily through economic and financial aid which is essential to economic stability and orderly political processes . . .

The seeds of totalitarian regimes are nurtured by misery and want. They spread and grow in the evil soil of poverty and strife. They reach their full growth when the hope of a people for a better life has died. We must keep that hope alive.

The free peoples of the world look to us for support in maintaining their freedoms.

If we falter in our leadership, we may endanger the peace of the world – and we shall surely endanger the welfare of our own nation.

Great responsibilities have been placed upon us by the swift movement of events.

I am confident that the Congress will face these responsibilities squarely.[11]

This was precisely the commitment from the USA Churchill had sought with the Fulton and Zurich speeches. In Missouri he had drawn the defining line between freedom and tyranny. Here it was stated once more with total clarity:

> One way of life is based upon the will of the majority . . .
> distinguished by free institutions, representative government, free
> elections, guarantees of individual liberty. The second way of life
> is based upon the will of a minority imposed upon the majority.
> It relies upon terror and oppression.[12]

At Fulton, Churchill had postulated 'two giant marauders'. To Congress, Truman recognised the effects of both tyranny and war. One robbed people of their rights and freedom. The other had 'dissolved the frame of civilized society' confronting 'humble folk with difficulties with which they cannot cope'. For them, 'all is distorted, all is broken, even ground to pulp'. At Zurich this was precisely the state of Europe as Churchill saw it. 'Over wide areas,' he lamented, 'a vast quivering mass of tormented, hungry, care worn, and bewildered human beings gape at the ruins of their cities and hopes.' This was 'the tragedy of Europe' which had to be addressed and only the Americans had the resources. Here then, to his immense relief, the USA under Truman was now ready to act, calling on Congress to provide 'the economic and financial aid . . . essential to economic stability and orderly political processes'.

And the reason? Again he echoed Churchill:

> The seeds of totalitarian regimes are nurtured by misery and
> want. They spread and grow in the evil soil of poverty and strife.
> They reach their full growth when the hope of a people for a
> better life has died. We must keep that hope alive.

His analysis was also identical to that of Marshall, so shocked by Stalin's indifference to the conditions in Germany. The Marshall Plan would do more than keep the hope alive. It would kick start economic growth and recovery. Above all it would restart the motors of economic power in France and Germany, replacing poverty and strife with the Franco-German partnership called for by Churchill in Zurich and later realised in the Coal and Steel Community linking both nations.

Truman ended his address to Congress by accepting the Churchillian challenge to pick up the mantle of Western leadership now so far beyond Britain's resources. He drew a line so clear, firm and determined that even Stalin must heed it. He declared to Congress and to the world: 'I believe it must be the policy of the United States to support free peoples who are resisting attempted subjugation by armed minorities or by outside pressures.' There were no 'ifs' or 'buts'; Truman was unequivocal. His determination would be sorely and dangerously tested ultimately in Berlin.

However, the immediate crisis resulted from British economic exhaustion and its consequences. These constituted the second unavoidable challenge to the USA forcing its change from irritation with Russia to a robust determination to contain Soviet ambition and defeat Russian expansion. Washington had been informed by London that it would have to evacuate British forces from Greece as it no longer had the means to counter communist guerrilla forces there. Now fully alert to the nature of Soviet ambitions and the methods by which it could impose its 'social system' the Americans were confronted with the undeniable reality of British weakness. After explaining this to Congress, Truman asked and received authorisation to provide Greece and Turkey with $400 million in economic wealth and military assistance.

To George C. Marshall, what was involved was nothing less than the opening move by Russia to secure their domination in Europe, the Middle East and Asia. His analysis was stark:

> If Greece should dissolve into civil war it is altogether probable that it would emerge as a Communist state under Soviet control. Turkey would be surrounded . . . Soviet domination might thus extend over the entire Middle East to the borders of India. The effect of this upon . . . Austria, Italy, and France cannot be overestimated. It is not alarmist to say that we are faced with the first crisis of a series which might extend Soviet domination to Europe, the Middle East, and Asia.[13]

In the event Marshall was being uncharacteristically alarmist. In part this was because the aid package of $400 million proved effective. In part it was because the crisis in the Aegean was on the periphery of the tightening confrontation between the USSR and the West.

Another decisive clash was about to occur at the very centre of Europe – Berlin. Its outcome would prove disastrous for Stalin and the USSR. In retrospect, Stalin's blockade of Berlin can be seen as a last throw at wresting back the initiative from the Americans and the West. By the time the blockade was lifted in May 1949, the Marshall Plan was under way. The North Atlantic Treaty had been signed in April and ratified in the US Senate by eighty-two votes to thirteen, and the Basic Law creating the Federal Republic of Germany had cleared all its hurdles with elections scheduled for August the same year. In October, Truman was elected for his second term. In his biography of the president, Roy Jenkins quotes Mrs Truman's comment as they returned to the White House, with sore throats but the vote in the bag: 'it looks like you're going to have to put up with us for another four years'.

They would be a difficult four years plagued by the visceral witch hunting of suspected communists led by Joe McCarthy and followed by a Republican victory bringing General Eisenhower to the White House and Foster Dulles to the State Department. This development posed a problem for Winston Churchill who would find himself back in Downing Street as prime minister. Yet none of this can or should distract from the extraordinary turning of the tide in the Cold War in 1947, 1948 and 1949 – a metamorphosis in part enabled by Churchill's impact in 1946.

Pivotal was the Berlin blockade and its outcome. That the Western Allies – the USA, Britain and France – were able to keep Berliners heated and fed from June 1948 to May 1949 in an airlift in which Allied planes were landing, on average, every ninety seconds, carrying fuel and food, and flying along restricted air corridors that were the only lines of supply for over two million beleaguered women, men and children, was a triumph of logistics, airmanship and courage. It was also an awesome political achievement. The air forces that had devastated wartime Berlin now saved it. They did so with the support of the US Congress, the British Parliament and the French government. Churchill's speech of 1946 played a significant part in this – alerting political and public opinion to the true nature of 'good old Uncle Joe', the reality of the Iron Curtain and the imperative for an Atlantic alliance capable of containing Russia.

Why had Stalin ordered the blockade? He was faced with the US initiatives to deny him his ambition for Germany as a bridgehead to wider domination. He believed, as had Lenin, that Germany and its proletariat was the key to opening continental Western Europe to communist control. Communist support in France, Italy and Greece was important but would not be decisive. In any case the appeal of these parties would be eroded by prosperity and the impact of the Marshall Plan. If the same changes swept Berlin and Western Germany, if a new West denied him German reparations, if the Western zones of Germany successfully merged and a democratic federal republic emerged, then he would be thwarted.

As we have noted, on being told by Truman in Potsdam of the advent of the atomic bomb, Stalin had told Zhukov and Gromyko that he believed Britain and America wished to force the USSR to accept their plans during the time it would take to build a Soviet bomb. He assured them 'that's not going to happen'. To gain control of all Berlin seemed the best way to ensure that what he feared 'was not going to happen'. It was dramatic, dangerous, ruthless, and in the event it failed.

One extraordinary dimension to Stalin's gamble and Western resolve turned on the critical duration of America's temporary atomic monopoly. During the airlift and at Britain's request B29s were flown to the UK. They would have been able to reach Russia, but they were not as yet equipped to carry atomic bombs even if such weapons were available. Their production lagged way behind expectations.

Nevertheless sixty B29s reached England in July 1947. British and American determination was hardening. According to Marshall's biographer, Forrest Pogue, British Foreign Secretary Ernest Bevin judged that 'the abandonment of Berlin would mean the loss of Western Europe'. The West had to break the blockade. Marshall was hugely encouraged by the swing in US public opinion. He declared 'from all reports the country is more unified in its determination not to weaken in the face of the pressure of an illegal blockade than on any other issue we can recall in time of peace'.[14]

Yet American confidence still ultimately relied on its bomb – the weapon that balanced the Soviets' huge superiority on the ground in Central Europe. They did believe it would take years for Russia to develop its weapon. Stalin was right in the analysis he gave Zhukov and Molotov. Washington probably thought it would take up to six years. They underestimated Beria's energy and the effectiveness of Stalin's terror to accelerate his nuclear programme. The West's monopoly held out throughout the crucial winter of 1947–8 as Western supplies kept Berlin alive. Yet the outcome was so perilous that the White House had directly to confront the issue of whether to use the bomb if all seemed lost. Truman said he prayed he would not have to make such a decision but that if it became necessary they should have 'no doubt' about his decision.[15]

Fortunately he never had to. The Soviets successfully tested their first atomic bomb on 29 August 1949. By then any hope of strangling Berlin had gone. The Berlin blockade had been lifted on 12 May – three months earlier. In September, Stalin went on a three-month holiday. The USA's journey from irritation to determination had reached its decisive destination. Stalin never recovered the initiative in Europe.

PART VI

Winners and Losers

19

How and Why the Impact?

How did Churchill pull it off? In the aftermath of personal defeat
and at the zenith of Soviet power, Churchill succeeded in creating
a new beginning for the West and ultimately the world. There
were three reasons.

First, no one could stop him. He was not prime minister. He
was not bound by either Parliament or the civil service. Although
Attlee's support was guarded, and Truman distanced himself
dramatically, they both wished and willed Churchill to act.
Attlee needed him to exploit his unique status in the USA to
achieve the financial loan to Britain. Truman was alert to the
Soviet threat and closely informed by George Kennan and
General Marshall. Domestically he was not strong enough to
challenge the Roosevelt legacy of 'good old Uncle Joe', but
despite this Truman would not stop Churchill and in any case
he could not have done so. On the British side, Ernest Bevin
welcomed Churchill's call to arms. He was deeply alarmed by
the Soviet threat and resolutely anti-communist because of his
trade-union experience.

Second, if the above constituted a kind of mandate, Churchill's
personal travail provided a substantial part of his motivation. After
the election he believed he had lost the power to shape events. He
had plummeted from the stratosphere at which he was happiest.

However, Fulton and Zurich proved that he still had the power to take the initiative in constructing a new Atlantic alliance.

Third, uniquely, he had the celebrity status to command a global audience and make a difference. His credibility was based on having been the only statesman to get it right in 1940 and to have inspired Britain to stand alone against Hitler.

Essential to Winston Churchill's ability to seize the hem of history in 1946, despite his lack of office, was his understanding and command of the power of the word. He believed that words can shape the world, alter the course of events and even determine the success or failure of nations at critical moments. He also believed from personal experience that the power of the word can do the same for the individual. To him, his career would have been inconceivable and unrealisable without his success with both the written and spoken word.

The written word was for him the easier medium. His writings were prolific – in his lifetime no fewer than forty-three books and many thousands of articles. The Nobel Prize for Literature in 1953 would be one of his most valued awards. He wrote to promote his beliefs, to warn of the worst and encourage the best of what he could see and foresee. He also wrote to defend his reputation – acutely aware that he could rely only on his own pen to ultimately achieve this. His accounts of the two world wars, so very different, share this characteristic: it was vital to persuade present and future generations to see the past as he did.[1]

He also used his power with words to make a living – as he often reminded people. In the hard times between the wars, having lost much money in the crisis of capitalism starting with the Great Crash of 1929 and having lost office for much of the period, his lifestyle – aristocratic and sybaritic – could only be sustained by his outpouring of words. He was fortunate but also astute in

identifying those who would pay well. Lord Beaverbrook, so
pivotal to Churchill in war, was also crucial to him in peacetime
helping to ensure, by commissioning his journalism, that he
could remain satisfied with the very best. Churchill's hospitality,
Chartwell itself, the wines, the food, the cigars and the ambiance
of great success especially when it eluded him, was not only
essential to his own morale, but vital in persuading others of his
relevance and potential. It was his stage.

He loved the English language – cherished it, revelled in it,
pursued its power to communicate with passion and dedication. It
was this commitment to identifying the right words and phrases
that could enchant him but also exhilarate him. He was an athlete
with the written word – exacting of himself and the secretaries
who became so essential to his writing and his speaking.

The written word was the bridge for him to the spoken word.
A natural writer, he was not a natural orator. As an MP he learnt
early that being unprepared meant he could be unsuccessful. His
maiden speech on 18 February 1901 was well regarded. Some of
his later speeches – less well worked on – were judged vacuous
and ineffective.

How he learned to command the spoken word – which he was
to do so irreplaceably in 1940 and later so powerfully in 1946 –
involved him in the considered choice of every word he deployed.
Nowhere is this better demonstrated than in the drafts of speeches
now kept at the Churchill Archives at Cambridge.

For me, this is especially so in the text of his broadcast on
17 June 1940 following France's capitulation. What rivets one's
attention are Churchill's handwritten alterations. The typed text
had read: 'What has happened in France makes no difference to
our actions and purpose.' But Churchill had the realism to look
into the abyss as well as the courage to bridge it. He knew only

too well how the fall of France must affect British actions. With his pen he strikes out 'no', and tries 'some', and then 'little'. But this makes the sentence equivocal, uncertain. The purpose of the speech is to engender courage, defiance and hope. So Churchill restores his original 'no' but changes 'actions' to 'faith'. The sentence is now armed to be sent into battle. It reads: 'What has happened in France makes no difference to our faith and purpose.' The archival evidence would seem to suggest that Churchill made these changes at the last minute, as the un-amended text was already in circulation. The recording of the broadcast reveals one further alteration. He replaced 'our' with 'British'.

Churchill altered the text when describing Soviet ambition. He had written 'what they [Soviets] desire is the fruits of war and the undefined expansion of their power and doctrines'. He changed 'undefined' to 'indefinite' and stuck with the change. The realisation that the expansion of Soviet power would be opportunistic and only restricted by a reluctance to risk nuclear war was uniquely a Churchillian perspective.

At Zurich, Churchill altered his text from the general to the specific. He talked of re-creating the European family and providing it with a structure under which it can dwell in peace, safety and freedom. Then, by hand, he added the sentence 'we must build a kind of United States of Europe'. This phrase has become the cause of confusion and controversy in Britain and in particular amongst British right-wing Conservatives, even today. In fact, the speech makes it clear that he sees this being led by a partnership between France and Germany with Britain in full support, but not with membership.

The second alteration, on page 7, is a matter of drama and delivery. His original text says 'I am going to say something that will astonish you', but after 'I am' he added 'NOW'. And indeed it did astonish. It is Churchill's sense of the moment and the power of rhetoric to define it. A call to arms and a sense of urgency is brought to what he is about to say.

That these wartime speeches – so alive and powerful within these Archives – changed the course of the war is clear. British morale did not collapse, neither in 1940 nor during the Blitz. Churchill's words met the supreme challenge to democratic leadership at a time of ultimate crisis. They made free people brave. They steadied nerves and stiffened resolution. They built the conviction that Britain's cause was right and would ultimately triumph.

In January 2006 an obituary appeared in the *Daily Telegraph*. It was of Iris 'Fluff' Bower, an RAF nurse bombed out twice, her husband killed in action only a year after their marriage. She went on to land with the first British troops on Juno Beach on 12 June 1944, and to serve with distinction to the end of the war. She volunteered for the service she gave. What was her motivation? She wrote:'I had a strong feeling that what we were taking part in was grand and noble.'[2]

Bower did not mention Churchill or his speeches but it was their purpose to persuade the British that their cause was 'grand and noble' and they succeeded. Churchill's words could and did reshape opinion.

The poet A. P. Herbert, on first hearing one of Churchill's wartime broadcasts, wrote that his impact was 'like an organ filling a church, sending the congregation refreshed and resolute to do or die'.[3]

This judgement that his speeches changed opinion has been challenged most recently by Professor Richard Toye. The organisation Mass Observation, which attempted to track British public opinion during the Second World War, found that there were those who thought Churchill's broadcast speeches 'depressing' and 'suspected he was either lying or quite simply drunk'.[4] However, Mass Observation never measured how many people held such views. By contrast, Gallup did and, as the eminent pollster Peter Kellner has pointed out in the British Press, only rarely did Churchill's oratory fail to win an approval rating of 80 per cent or more despite the often bleak messages he had to convey.

David Cannadine, in his excellent and perceptive introduction to *The Speeches of Winston Churchill*, begins with a sentence that sums up the paradox of Churchill's oratory. He writes, 'Winston Churchill was the most eloquent and expressive statesman of his time, truly both the master and the slave of the English language',[5] and 'it was as an orator that Churchill became the most fully and completely alive and it was through his oratory that his words and his phrases made their greatest and most enduring impact'.[6]

But his speeches didn't win him Number 10. In fact, his infamous attack on Labour's 'Gestapo' helped him lose the 1945 election. So what were the weaknesses in Churchill's oratory? Cannadine identifies three.

First, that

the very luxuriance of his rhetoric . . . so readily mobilised in support of so many and even contradictory causes only served to reinforce the view – which became widespread . . . that he was a man of unstable temperament and defective judgement, completely lacking in any real sense of proportion.[7]

Undeniably in 1940 and again in 1946 'he mobilised the English language' and sent it into battle for freedom. But he also mobilised it to battle for the doomed Prince of Wales before his abdication, to denounce Gandhi (now on a plinth with him in Parliament Square), to attack the Tories of whom he had been so conspicuous a member and then to advocate the Liberal cause only to abandon it as well. His rhetoric was harnessed to 'ratting and re-ratting', as he put it.

Second, Cannadine quotes Charles Masterman's scathing complaint that Churchill 'can convince himself of almost every truth if it is once allowed to start on its wild career through his rhetorical machinery!'[8]

Third, his rhetoric was often ill-suited for the stage he cared most about – the floor of the House of Commons. Cannadine recounts Attlee's verdict. While Churchill's parliamentary speeches were often 'magnificent rhetorical performances' they were frequently 'too stately, too pompous, and too elaborate to be ideal House of Commons stuff'.[9]

Churchill's wit and sarcasm could be lethal – his dismissal of Attlee's modesty as a recognition that he had much to be modest about is well known, as is the occasion for it. His repartee was not only devastating when directed at his opponents. It could be directed against anyone who annoyed him. My own favourite story to illustrate how devastating his retorts could be relates to his occupancy of the headquarters of the English Speaking Union, at 37 Charles Street in the heart of Mayfair. He was its chairman which gave him rooms at a most desirable address and invitations to exclusive dinners.

On one occasion Churchill was greeted by the wealthy lady occupant at the door only to be told by her that she had invited too many men for the number of women attending. Churchill was dismayed and commented that he understood that 'the purpose of this evening was to dine, not to breed.' It was, of course, a brilliant retort and probably spontaneous, but spontaneity was not his forte. He prepared and rehearsed his wit as tirelessly as all other aspects of his rhetoric – as Attlee too

commented on this characteristic that his humour was 'too elaborate to be ideal House of Commons stuff'.

Overall, Churchill's grasp of 'the power of the word' was over-
whelmingly effective. He turned his lisp into a distinctive
characteristic. It became part of his brand. Largely self-educated,
he drew thirstily from the wells of his own reading – Gladstone,
the Younger Pitt, and as a subaltern stationed in India, the
cadences of Gibbon and 'the pungent wit of Macaulay'.[10]

However, one man – unexpected and unlikely – seems to have
had more influence in shaping the style, discipline and panache of
his rhetoric than any other – an Irish-American Congressman by
the name of Bourke Cockran.

When visiting Fulton, Missouri in late January 2015 to attend
and participate in a service in the Wren Church blitzed by the
Germans in 1940 and transported across the Atlantic and rebuilt in
Fulton to commemorate Churchill after his death in 1965, I
encountered a namesake, Baxter Brown Watson.

When Churchill spoke at Fulton in 1946, Baxter Brown
Watson, then a young student, was chosen to lead the procession
of Churchill and President Truman into the gymnasium where he
spoke and which still stands substantially unaltered. At a lunch
after the service attended by Britain's ambassador to Washington,
the young Duncan Sandys, as well as the artist Edwina Sandys, I
sat next to Watson, now a spruce man in his nineties with a lively
and accurate memory. I asked him what the audience in the
gymnasium had made of Churchill's rhetoric back on 5 March
1946. He replied:

It went straight over their heads. They hung on every word because this was truly a great man. He was famous everywhere
and here he was, in Fulton. It was a unique moment – the most

important in Fulton's history and that of the college. We were part of it and it made the hairs on the back of your neck stand up. We may not have understood the speech but my God we knew it mattered!

We struck up a lengthy, illuminating conversation. Watson enquired whether I really knew who had most influenced Churchill's rhetoric. Who had been the person on whom he modelled his style? Did I know who had taught Churchill that words can sing? It was, he assured me, Congressman Bourke Cockran, and had heard this confirmed many times. I had read a little of Bourke Cockran but not grasped his significance. Watson had made it the study of a lifetime. He explained that he wished to entrust this research to me because he believed it would be crucial to my undertaking of Churchill's world-shaping oratory. Before I left Fulton he deposited a hefty folder for me at the front desk of the Churchill Museum in the undercroft of Fulton's unlikely Christopher Wren parish church.

The contents of the folder did not contain any original papers but Watson had meticulously collected all published sources about Bourke Cockran and collectively they have proved a rich vein of resource for which I am indebted to him.

The first and cardinal fact is that the Irish-American, in the words of Roy Jenkins, 'had undoubtedly been one of Churchill's mother's most successful admirers'.[11] Or, as author Richard Holmes expressed it more bluntly, 'one of Jennie's oldest and most durable lovers'.[12] Their assignation had begun, according to Ralph Martin's account in *Jennie: The Life of Lady Randolph Churchill*, at a dinner in Paris at 34 Avenue Kleber in March 1895. He tells us that 'the attraction was quick and mutual . . . they were free enough to do as they pleased, adult enough to know what they wanted in this summer of their lives'.[13]

Whatever the veracity or accuracy of all this, what is quite clear is that Churchill's mother trusted Cockran to act as her son's host and mentor when Winston first arrived in New York in November 1895 on his way to Cuba. He had five months' leave before his posting to India and he intended to use it to see and report on war – in this case the Spanish government's determined attempt to suppress rebellion in Cuba. His route of travel had to be via New York and it was to Cockran that his mother wrote, asking him to host her son. He readily agreed and was on the quayside to greet the young Churchill and his friend Barnes, another subaltern destined for India.

Churchill was an eager visitor, hugely excited by the glamour, brashness and energy of New York.

Cockran was a splendid host, doubtless in part motivated by his devotion to Jennie and their love affair which had started only six weeks earlier. He lavishly entertained and hosted the two young Englishmen at his quite luxurious apartment at 713 West Avenue. He shared his best cognacs and introduced Winston to his finest Havana cigars – a taste that would be enhanced in Cuba and give him great pleasure for the rest of his life.

Much more important than Cockran's generosity was his advice. Churchill wrote later: 'I must record the strong impression that this remarkable man made upon my untutored mind. I have never seen his like or in some respects his equal.'[14]

Richard Holmes perhaps touches the heart of the matter. Cockran had become intimate with Lady Randolph Churchill after the death of her husband. He may have 'helped fill the void left by the death of Lord Randolph'[15] for his son.

What is clear is that Cockran pulled aside a curtain of understanding for Churchill. As Randolph Churchill, Winston's son, ratifies in his biography of his father, Cockran was 'the first man or woman Churchill met on level terms who really saw his point and potentialities'.[16]

Yet what matters most in evaluating Churchill's grasp of the power of the word was what he learnt from Cockran about presence, delivery and the drama of speech. The US presidential candidate Adlai Stevenson recalled how Winston had confided to him that Cockran had been 'the mould on which he based his oratorical style. Bourke Cockran taught me to use every note of the human voice as if playing an organ.' Churchill then quoted long passages of Bourke's speeches and ended by admitting that is was he who 'was my model. I learned from him how to hold thousands in thrall.'[17]

One of the reasons why Churchill's two speeches in 1946 do not suffer from the weaknesses that he had evidenced again in the House of Commons as Leader of the Opposition in 1946 was simply that the task of being Leader of the Opposition bored him, whereas he was exhilarated by the challenge of the Fulton and Zurich speeches. Here he was able to match the moment with his rhetoric.

This rhetoric may have gone over the heads of his audience in the gymnasium at Fulton, and escaped the full understanding of the professors and VIPs in the hall at Zurich University, but the nuclear centre of Churchill's oratory was his professionalism, his accuracy, his command of the word.

Churchill was not only a prolific author and unique orator, he also had a profound understanding of the media and how to use it. He had started his career as a journalist. He made his name by writing dramatic accounts of his experiences in battle and war – in Cuba, on the Indian frontier and above all in South Africa. He built his own profile and as was commented at the time, his history of the First World War – *The World Crisis* – was essentially a history of his own participation in it. He did believe that his own history was too important to be left to others.

He consumed newspapers as well as contributing to them. His friendship with Beaverbrook was not only legendary but lucrative for Churchill. His lifestyle, which far exceeded his means during the interwar period, depended on the earning power of his pen.

The two world wars engendered a global press and Churchill well understood this. He exploited the way in which he was depicted. His personal branding was the equal of Charlie Chaplin's. The V sign, the Homburg hat, the bow tie, the cigar. All these were multiplied endlessly across newspapers and increasingly in the newsreels which also became global during the period. Churchill also mastered radio. He ensured that both Fulton and Zurich were broadcast worldwide and fully covered by newsreels.

He never accommodated television but no doubt if he'd lived in a different age, he would have done so. Certainly his funeral contained one of the most famous television pictures of all time – the cranes of the port of London bowing in respect.

Motivation, mandate, professionalism, media. None would have ensured the coup of 1946 without Churchill's grasp of the moment and the meaning of history in the making. Like Bismarck he believed in grasping the mantle of history. It was his sense of moment that transformed the banality of the gymnasium in Fulton into the fulcrum of the new alliance architecture. It was his sense of the moment and its drama that enabled him to tell his rather dull audience in Zurich 'I will surprise you' and then to shock them beyond measure by suggesting a partnership of leadership between France and Germany.

Perspective

This is a tale full of giants – some malevolent like Stalin, some blessed with extraordinary talent and spirit of which Churchill is the exemplar. It was he who remarked that while we are all worms, he was a glow worm. There is Harry S. Truman – initially an unexpected, unwanted and underrated president of the United States who emerges as 'the first President to preside over Pax Americana'.[1] There are smaller men who nonetheless strut this stage – Lord Halifax, ever sceptical of Churchill's judgement, and Anthony Eden, ever envious of Churchill's occupancy of Number 10. There is Molotov, ever ready with a '*Niet*', and George C. Marshall, ever ready with a solution. And many others too. But towering above them all is Churchill – a man of unique dimensions of character, a man who not only grasped the hem of history, but wrapped himself in its mantle. As written so memorably by Isaiah Berlin, Churchill was 'the largest human being of our time'.[2]

Thus, in retrospect, we should look at the key players in judging who were the winners and losers in this journey that changed Churchill and the world. Who were they?

The focus of this book has been Churchill's role in 1946. Assuring his achievement in 'smiting the crocodile' with his two speeches at Fulton and Zurich, one can thus ask of the three giants – Stalin, Truman and Churchill – to what extent each emerged a winner or a loser.

Stalin lost the initiative his wartime victory had seemed to confer. In July 1945 he travelled to Potsdam in an armoured train guarded all the way along a near 2000 kilometre route by thousands of NKVD forces. In his report to Stalin on the arrangements for the journey, Beria details where they are to be deployed. It gives us a dramatic glimpse of the empire Stalin had at his feet. 'To provide proper security,' he wrote, '1515 NKVDIGB men of operative staff and 17,409 NKVD forces are placed in the following order: on USSR territories – 6 men per kilometer; on Polish territory – 10 men per kilometer, on German territory – 15 men per kilometer.'[3] The day after Stalin arrived in Potsdam – 16 July – the USA successfully tested its first A-bomb. At Yalta, earlier at Tehran and now at Potsdam, Stalin would seem to get all he wanted. But the atomic bomb provided the window of opportunity that Churchill so brilliantly exploited in the year that followed.

That by June 1948 Stalin had decided to start his blockade of Berlin provides the measure of how his victory had been diminished and its potential eroded. Churchill's speeches were key to this process. As we have seen they revealed Uncle Joe for the tyrant and threat he was and by alerting the USA and Europe to the imperative of a new alliance they thwarted Soviet ambition. The blockade was Stalin's last chance to counter the momentum of the West. It seems that one reason why he thought he might pull it off was the Nazi failure to reinforce the Wehrmacht in Stalingrad during their siege of that city. Stalin's failure to understand the realities of the Berlin airlift is powerfully demonstrated by the idea that because Goering could not save Paulus's 6th army in 1942 the US Air Force and the RAF could not save Berlin in 1948.

In his last years Stalin was imprisoned by this unreality. His paranoia and megalomania consumed him. His ruthlessness and cynicism grew into cancers that destroyed him. He outmanoeuvred all those who hoped to succeed him, terrifying them at party meetings, tricking them into charge and counter-charge, having unknown numbers, high and low, purged, tortured and killed. He planned and began an anti-Semitic terror against the alleged Jewish doctors conspiracy, which had he not died in 1953, would have imitated Hitler's cruelty. Both men relished violence and enjoyed the details of the brutalities they ordered, from Stalin's red hot irons applied by the NKVD in torture cells to Hitler's gratification in having the death throes of those involved in the July plot and hung by piano wire at Plötzensee filmed for him to view.

Stalin was not only thwarted in Europe. His cynical misleading of Mao and the North Koreans in the Korean War availed him nothing. Stalin was happy to see the North Koreans fight to their last man but it was Truman's skill at the United Nations that ensured the West could fight to defend South Korea as a UN force and succeed.

When Stalin first met Truman he was not impressed. This was not a man he would lose out to in any contest. He judged Truman to be 'neither educated nor clever', in no way to be compared to Roosevelt. This first encounter took place at the Cecilienhof in Potsdam on 17 July 1945. Within hours, however, Stalin was confronted with a directness, a sharpness he had never experienced with Roosevelt.

Truman led off their first plenary session. Around a table engulfed in tobacco smoke from Churchill's cigars and Stalin's cigarettes, Truman rejected any obfuscation. Looking directly at Stalin he read from a prepared statement. It addressed Stalin's failure to deliver the promises he had given at the Yalta conference. Churchill as well as Stalin was taken aback. Here was a new, untested US president, virtually unknown and not present at Yalta, accusing the Russians of bad faith. 'Since the Yalta conference,' he declared, 'the obligations undertaken in the declaration on liberated Europe remain unfulfilled. In conformity with these obligations . . . the Governments of the three powers must discuss how best to help the work of the provisional Governments in holding free and fair elections.' He then listed the causes of his concern: 'Such help,' he explained, 'will be required in Romania, Bulgaria and possibly other countries too.' Stalin said nothing. Truman pressed on with his agenda. He asserted it was important to admit Italy to the United Nations. Churchill could not contain himself. These were matters too important to be dealt with 'somewhat too hastily'.[4] Within minutes of the Potsdam Conference getting under way the 'natty' former haberdasher from Missouri, immaculate in his double-breasted suit, had astonished Churchill and Stalin both resplendent in their military uniforms. The newcomer was focused, bold, energetic – so very different from the ailing Roosevelt at Yalta. His sharpness was evident in his face – eyes bright and level behind no-nonsense, steel-rimmed glasses. His manner was entirely new. At the end of their first session, he insisted that they 'specify the concrete questions for discussion' the next day. Churchill argued that their secretaries could give them enough points 'to keep us busy'. Truman's riposte was a challenge: 'I don't want to discuss. I want to decide.' He added that 'our sittings should start at four o'clock instead of five'. Clearly puzzled, Stalin conceded with 'Well, all right' and Churchill with the ironic 'I will obey your orders'.[5]

Churchill was ambiguous about the new president expressing both positive and negative views. Despite Truman's inexperience, however, Churchill understood that the new president was reorganising the reality of the US–USSR relationship. Much later Churchill admitted to Truman that at Potsdam he had misjudged him. He then paid the president the greatest compliment he could express. Since their first meeting when he had misjudged him so badly, he had come to recognise that Truman 'more than any other man'[6] had saved Western civilisation. Given Churchill's own contribution to that cause, it was an awesome tribute.

Churchill's admiration for Truman grew steadily during his presidency but there were difficult episodes. There was the shock of Truman's abrupt cessation of Lend-Lease the moment the war ended. The USA could afford its aid to Britain. Its industries were intact, while Britain's were damaged by bombing and almost entirely given over to war production. Suddenly America's financial and material support vanished. Unless it was resumed the UK faced bankruptcy – a cruel reward for British courage.

That was how Churchill saw it. When America did offer a loan of $3,750 million the terms were harsh and, as we have seen, led Churchill to abstain when the House of Commons voted on them.

Then when Churchill gave his Fulton speech there was Truman's strange behaviour in denying any knowledge of its contents and distancing himself publicly from its case proposed for a powerful Anglo-American alliance. Privately, Churchill took some offence noting that the newsreels showed Truman applauding the idea as Churchill spoke at Westminster College. However, he must have recognised the 'realpolitik' determining Truman's actions. Truman's intent in urging Churchill to give his Fulton speech was to alert Americans to the Soviet threat. He was not – at that moment – prepared to commit to a new alliance with Britain. In reality, he needed Churchill to do his work for him in preparing public opinion.

Truman's own direct appeal to the American public came a year later in his address to Congress on 12 March 1947. Truman saw this as 'America's answer to the surge of expansion of Communist tyranny'. In his own account of the writing of this speech, he made clear that he wanted 'no hedging in this speech'. The doctrine he expounded had to be 'clear and free of hesitation or double talk'.[7] It was and its clarity echoed his bluntness of Potsdam on the first day of that conference in warning Stalin directly that he was in breach of the commitments he had given at Yalta.

In a fascinating study of the Truman Doctrine speech, Duke University provides the polling evidence of how Truman jolted Americans into much greater awareness of the threat facing the West. It cites the polls showing that following the end of the war only 7 per cent of Americans named 'foreign problems' as giving them any concern. After all they had just won the war. Following Truman's speech on 12 March 1947, the figure rose to 54 per cent. This swing in public mood was to be essential in the confrontation with Stalin over Berlin. However, it was Churchill who started the process. In the summer of 1946, the percentage of Americans rating foreign problems as 'most important' reached and stayed above 20 per cent – not high, but rising.

The reality was that both Churchill and Truman were up against an understandable American preference for peace. Congress was hostile to the taxation and conscription implications of an alliance to opposing Russia. Without Truman's clarity and firmness the Berlin airlift could not have been mounted in the weeks before it began. Truman confronted the risk of war. He was unequivocal: 'We would have to deal with the situation as it developed.'[8]

Was Truman a winner or a loser? He was indeed the first president of the Pax Americana. He committed the power of the United States to a policy of active containment of communist aggression. Berlin did not fall. Neither did South Korea. And he won a second term in the White House. Underestimated at the start by Stalin, Churchill and the US public, Truman emerges a winner.

When Stalin died in 1953 his daughter Svetlana was in the room. She described the scene. 'He literally choked to death . . . the death agony was terrible . . . at the last minute he opened his eyes . . . it was a terrible look, either mad or angry and full of the fear of death.'[9] He suffered the fate he had ordered for so many. For all his power and cunning, Stalin was a loser.

On Truman's side he never doubted the stature of Churchill. In the judgement of Roy Jenkins's biography of Truman, the president 'had come to adore Churchill'. When Churchill died in January 1965, Truman's tribute was characteristically pithy and to the point. Churchill, he said, 'typified man's resolution to be free'.[10]

As this book has sought to demonstrate, Churchill's ultimate motivation and objective was the defence of liberty against tyranny. Clearly he was not the loser for had he lost in 1940, his country's freedom and that of Western Europe would have been extinguished – perhaps for centuries. What he achieved in 1946 was also critical for the defence of liberty against tyranny. So against his own measure, Churchill was a winner.

Yet the balance of success and failure is – in his case – a drama of light and dark. At his funeral in 1965, the mood was of loss – not only of the man but also of the power and position of Britain itself. He had pledged that as the king's First Minister he would never preside over the dissolution of the Empire. By the time of his death, India had long been independent and the rest of the Empire would vanish in the decades to follow. His motivation was the defence of freedom but in his mind and heart Britain's freedom critically depended on the denial of independence to India and other parts of the Empire. Churchill the democrat and parliamentarian was also Churchill the imperialist. Far from conceding any contradiction in this, Churchill saw them as complementary. Roosevelt's enmity towards British imperialism irritated and frustrated Churchill almost as much as the president's naivety in dealing with Stalin.

Other paradoxes abound. Back on form, Churchill went on to win the general election. In October 1951 he again became prime minister, this time having beaten his opponents in an election. His majority in the House of Commons was thin – a mere seventeen MPs, but at the age of nearly seventy-seven it was a triumph, wiping out the bitter electoral defeat of 1945. Back then as one of the 'Big Three', Churchill at Potsdam still believed that if the West was strong and resolute, there could be peace within the USSR. His wartime summits persuaded him of the worth of summitry. Brought back from Potsdam by the voters, he now wanted to use his electoral mandate and his office as prime minister to persuade the Russians and Americans to return to the table. The risk of nuclear war – in his view – laid this obligation on the leaders of the USA, the USSR and the UK.

In this he would be frustrated – in part by a paradox. He and Truman had alerted the American public to the exterior threat posed to the USA by the communists. Fear of communism had by the time he was back in Number 10 swept the USA. Joe McCarthy whipped up a frenzy against communism as an internal enemy. Daily he denounced supposed communist sympathisers who would betray their country. As prime minister, Churchill arrived back in the USA to visit Truman in January 1952. He found 'an embittered and angry country'.[11] The Korean War and Stalin's role in it blighted any hope of a summit. Stalin's death seemed to

Churchill to offer a chance – a fresh hope. Then Eisenhower won the American election and with John Foster Dulles in the State Department, East–West relations entered 'a dead winter'.[12] Britain's waning strength and Churchill's declining health meant that any return to the top table as one of the 'Big Three' had become impossible. The leadership of the West had passed irreversibly to Washington.

There was another, for him, happier paradox that became evident during this later part of his life. On his visit to see Truman in 1952, he was invited to address Congress. He had perhaps thought to use the occasion to advocate summitry but he read the American mood correctly and focused on the Anglo-American alliance and, above all, on the language that bound the two nations together, 'working for the same high cause'. He put his case dramatically with these words:

> Bismarck once said that the supreme fact of the nineteenth cen-
> tury was that Britain and the US spoke the same language. Let us
> make sure that the supreme fact of the twentieth century is that
> they tread the same path.[13]

It was his command of that language that he deployed so effect-ively in 1940 but also in 1946. He had indeed armed the language and sent it into battle. He had given the lion's roar. The global reach of the language of which he was so accomplished a master was foreseen by him during the war.

In September 1943 he had received an honorary degree at Harvard University. He spoke of 'the priceless inheritance' of a common tongue shared by both nations. Looking forward to the war's end, he reflected on the unique role of English. It would be, he said, 'a grand convenience for us all to move freely about the world and be able to find everywhere a medium of intercourse and understanding'. That medium was English. Despite the end of empire and Britain's relative weakness, her language would become the world's second language. Its success was for him a source of pride and pleasure. One of the tributes paid to him at his death came from the first master of the Cambridge college founded in his honour. Sir John Cockcroft, Master of Churchill, wrote: 'So long as English is spoken and history studied, men will marvel at the greatness of Sir Winston Churchill and wonder that there could be such diversity in one man.'[14]

A winner or a loser? Of course the balance is clear and the beneficiary was the world. At Churchill's funeral in St Paul's, the then Archbishop of Canterbury thanked God 'for giving the world a man so great – a leader in conflict, in reconciliation, in humanity'.[15] The nature of his leadership during and after the war ensured that what the world could honour was not the end of an empire but the shape of a new world.

That had been the purpose of these two great speeches in Fulton and Zurich. Of him it was true – as T. S. Eliot expressed it in his poem 'East Coker' – 'In my end is my beginning.'

Afterword

While writing this book, the status of the speeches that are its subject has changed. In November 2015 the United Nations heritage body – UNESCO – determined that the Churchill Archives at Churchill College, Cambridge, including the drafts of his speeches, rank alongside the Magna Carta in the register of pivotal documents of world history.

They are recognised as a legacy left to mankind and in a special way to the English language and to the English-speaking peoples. This is of great importance to the Churchill Archives. They conserve our heritage, they illuminate and pass on Churchill's legacy to democracy itself.

Allen Packwood, the curator of the archives, has contributed a powerful appendix to this book explaining the significance of the archives and I testify to the invaluable contribution he and they have made to this work.

In 2015, Churchill's most prolific and influential historian, Sir Martin Gilbert, died. At his memorial service, Randolph Churchill spoke of his family's great debt to Sir Martin. Rabbi Lord Jonathan Sacks said that Gilbert had turned history into memory – he had made history part of how we think and feel not only about the past and present but also the future.

It is for this reason, above all, that Winston Churchill's speeches have become our legacy. They have changed our past, present and our future. They shape our understanding of freedom.

A cardinal dimension of this legacy is thus its relevance. This is demonstrated whenever contemporary statesmen invoke Churchill's memory as Prime Minister Cameron has over Syria. It is evidenced by the power of Churchill's example on politicians as varied as John F. Kennedy and Mikhail Gorbachev.

The relevance of Fulton and Zurich is particularly sharp today. Fulton laid upon the USA the responsibility to use its primacy of power to defend freedom. This burden still falls on America – especially as she grows more uncertain about her global status. She cannot withdraw from a dangerous world. As in 1946 isolationism remains an illusion. The United States has to engage with the challenges posed to democracy by Vladimir Putin in the Ukraine and by ISIS in the Middle East and terrorism across the globe.

The relevance of Zurich is also just as sharp. Europe 'led by' its core partnership of France and Germany must find its way through the confusion of both its refugee crisis and its currency chaos. It is still incumbent on them to seek 'a kind of United States of Europe'. It is equally incumbent on the UK to resist any temptation to succumb to its own version of isolation.

These two speeches – Fulton and Zurich – set out imperatives for today just as powerfully as when they were delivered in 1946. They are a vital part of Churchill's legacy to us. Part of our heritage. UNESCO's judgement endorses what we already know: that Churchill's speeches are crucial to our understanding of democracy.

In 1946, Churchill knew that he was not writing and speaking merely for the moment. His purpose was to shape the future – to startle, provoke and inspire Americans and Europeans into building a new alliance capable of securing democracy.

The care with which he chose every word and crafted every sentence is shown vividly by the pages of his original text reproduced in this book – his annotations, his decisions on what to include and what to exclude, his re-phrasings are all part of his legacy.

These facsimiles, published here for the first time, illustrate not only Churchill's professionalism but his determination to influence the thoughts and actions of free peoples in their future endeavours.

In this he succeeded. It is his legacy.

Letting Churchill Speak
A Note from Allen Packwood, Director of the Churchill Archives Centre, Churchill College, University of Cambridge

It is now over half a century since the death of Sir Winston Churchill, but as this excellent book has shown, his deeds and his words continue to echo down the years.

My whole career has been spent working in archives, and the last twenty years have been spent working on the Churchill Papers. To my mind, the importance and the power of these documents is twofold. First, they strip away the layers of hindsight and plunge you back into the mind-set of the past. It may in some ways be a different country, but once you have cracked the language, you are rewarded with a rich insight into how our predecessors saw their world, and why they took the decisions that continue to shape our lives today. Second, these archives help explain the making of our modern world, and it is only by understanding where we have come from that we will be able to shape where we are going.

On one very basic level of course Churchill's is just such an interesting life and he is just great fun. The first and most self-evident thing to say is that he lived his life to the full. As a young soldier and journalist he sought and found adventure, coming under fire in Cuba at the time of his twenty-first birthday, fighting the Pathans on the Indian North-West Frontier, charging the Dervishes at the Battle of Omdurman, and launching himself on the national and international stage with his daring escape from Boer captivity. He made his own luck, and then exploited it brilliantly by writing up his adventures as newspaper articles and books. It was a strategy that also underpinned his political career. Elected to Parliament at the age of just twenty-five, he was in the British cabinet aged thirty-three, and had already served as President of the Board of Trade, Home Secretary and First Lord of the Admiralty by the time of the outbreak of the First World War in 1914. He was no great respecter of party, beginning as a Conservative, but breaking with the Tories in 1904 to join the Liberal Party over the issue of free trade, only to return to the Conservatives again in 1924 over his opposition to socialism. Thereby apparently allowing him to remark that anyone could rat, but it took a certain ingenuity to re-rat.

From the outset, Churchill embraced controversy, and never seemed happier than when in the thick of the fray. He told the suffragettes he would not be henpecked, dismissed Gandhi as a 'half-naked fakir', likened the arrival of Lenin in Russia in a sealed train to the importation of a plague bacillus and dismissed Hitler as a squalid caucus butcher. He entered the House of Commons in 1900, taking up his seat in 1901, and left it in 1964, just short of his ninetieth birthday. And of course he was prime minister twice, and from 1940 to 1945 led his country through the great crisis of the Second World War. In the words of President Kennedy, who took them from Edward R. Murrow, who may have got them from Beverley Nichols, Churchill mobilised the English language and sent it into battle. During his lifetime he published some fifty books in some seventy volumes and won the Nobel Prize for

Literature. And I have not even mentioned the flying, the painting or the bricklaying.

So, there is such a wealth of great material to engage with, as is illustrated by the fact that his official biography runs to eight volumes, with companion volumes still being produced (though sadly no longer by Sir Martin Gilbert). This is a man who made history and wrote history.

This is reflected in the scale and complexity of his personal archive. The Churchill Papers are a wonderful resource. They are not a handful of papers, but rather a huge collection of almost three thousand boxes: an estimated one million pieces of paper. The collection was deliberately and systematically assembled by Sir Winston Churchill during his career, and includes everything from his childhood letters and school reports to his final writings. All sides of the man are represented: Churchill the writer in the drafts and manuscripts of his books and newspaper articles; Churchill the politician in his political and constituency correspondence; Churchill the minister in his official telegrams and minutes; Churchill the husband and father in his personal correspondence; and Churchill the orator in the annotated notes for the famous speeches. Together, this material makes a resource not just for the study of Churchill, but for the study of his era, and for the study of important international events and personalities from the imperial wars of the 1890s to the Cold War conflicts of the 1950s.

Why did Churchill assemble and keep this material? In part, he used his archive as a working resource. You only have to look at his multi-volume histories of the First and Second World Wars to see how he uses documents to tell his story. Of course, he uses them selectively. This after all is the man who joked in the House of Commons in 1948 that, 'For my part, I consider that it will be found much better by all Parties to leave the past to history, especially as I propose to write that history myself.'

There is no doubt that Churchill also had an eye to posterity and the judgement of history. He had written the biography of his own father, Lord Randolph Churchill, and lived to see his own son named as his chronicler. In the event, Randolph junior only survived to produce the first two volumes and the project was taken forward through eight volumes and related companion volumes by Sir Martin Gilbert. Churchill was aware of the value of his archive, both as a commercial and an academic resource, and he made provision for it when he came to settle his estate. The pre-1945 papers were assigned to the safekeeping of the Chartwell Trust, a family trust established with the intention of benefiting Churchill's direct line. The post-1945 papers were placed under the control of his wife, Clementine Spencer-Churchill.

The papers passed physically from father to son. After Randolph's death, they were given a temporary home at the Bodleian Library in Oxford, where Sir Martin Gilbert could access them from his base at Merton College. In the meantime, Churchill College had been built, and built as the National and Commonwealth Memorial to Sir Winston. From the time of its foundation in 1960, it began to acquire the papers of some of those who had worked in Churchill's inner circle. The first master, the Nobel Prize-winning physicist Sir John Cockcroft, Winston Churchill's confidant and former private secretary Sir John Colville and the naval historian Captain Stephen Roskill set about collecting a body of political, military, diplomatic and scientific papers relating to the 'Churchill Era'. In a letter of 14 July 1967, Cockcroft wrote:

> The aim of this venture is to make the College a major centre of historical research into what might be termed the Churchill

Era, where scholars will be able to find a great mass of inter-related material gathered together under a single roof.

Of course, the hope was always that Churchill's own papers would form the centrepiece of a new Churchill Archives Centre, and this dream came a step closer in 1969 when Lady Spencer-Churchill gave her husband's post-1945 papers to the college. A new building was purpose-built to house them, sitting at the heart of the Churchill College campus, and offering high-quality conservation, storage and reading-room facilities. The pre-1945 Churchill Papers arrived on deposit in 1974. They were still in the ownership of the Chartwell Trust, and were therefore described as the Chartwell Papers, as opposed to the post-1945 college-owned material that became known as the Churchill Papers. This is a somewhat confusing distinction that survives to this day in the reference codes for Churchill material. The pre-1945 papers all have the prefix CHAR; the post-1945 papers have the prefix CHUR.

Broadly speaking, this remained the position until April 1995 when, with the aid of a grant from the newly established Heritage Lottery Fund, the pre-1945 papers were purchased from the Chartwell Trust, securing the whole collection intact, in Britain, in perpetuity and vesting it all in a new charitable trust, the Sir Winston Churchill Archive Trust.

The pre- and post-1945 papers, now collectively known as the Churchill Papers, continue to be preserved in the Churchill Archives Centre, but on a completely different and fully open basis. Anyone can now consult the Churchill Papers and related collections in the Archives Centre reading rooms. Admission is free and the Centre is open from Monday to Friday, from 9am to 5pm.[1] Interested parties simply need to make an appointment.

The papers have also been conserved, packaged, microfilmed, exhibited and crucially digitised. The Centre has worked with the publisher Bloomsbury to make the collection freely available to all interested schools, and available by subscription to other universities and research institutes.[2]

The Churchill Papers now form the centrepiece, the jewel in the crown, of a wonderful collection of political, diplomatic, military and scientific papers at the Churchill Archives Centre. It is a huge honour to be their temporary custodian and enormously rewarding to see them used to support education, research and scholarship at all levels. The collection has inscription on the UNESCO Memory of the World Register, and the Centre has designation from the Museums, Libraries and Archives Council. Yet, the mission remains the same, to preserve the material for future generations, and to make it as widely available as possible. I am grateful to Alan Watson for his passionate interest in our material and for helping the Churchill Papers to fulfil their potential.

The degree of co-operation between an author and the archive is well demonstrated by this volume. Alan Watson has worked with the archive since the inception of his book. He has drawn extensively on the archives themselves and we have joined in debate and discussion of the direction of the book. The two speeches at Fulton and Zurich now share in the status conferred on Churchill's speeches by UNESCO. They are recognised as part of the chronicle of democracy as much as Magna Carta of centuries gone by. It is thus appropriate that of all Churchill's speeches these are the first two to become the subject of a special study since UNESCO's decision.

Acknowledgements

In writing this book I have benefitted throughout from the perspective, advice and assistance of Allen Packwood, Director of the Churchill Archives Centre, Churchill College, University of Cambridge. It was his wise counsel that I should widen my focus from Churchill's Fulton speech to include his Zurich speech and the relationship between both events. My visits to the Archives and those of my researchers have been much facilitated by the hospitality of the College and I am indebted to the Master and Fellows for their friendship and support, especially that of Dr Warren Dockter.

This book could not have been completed without the skill and dedication of my assistant Caroline Mouflard whose enthusiasm, accuracy and good judgement have been of invaluable help.

Two people have laboured for me in researching material online and in the archive – Professor Andra Alexandru and Professor Asya Rogova. For their alertness, tenacity and commitment I am much in their debt.

So too am I to my publisher, Bloomsbury – to its Chairman Nigel Newton for his timely encouragement, to Stephanie Duncan for her guidance and enthusiasm and to my editor Miranda Vaughan Jones for her painstaking liaison with Caroline and myself.

In New York, I benefitted also from Professor Jennifer Gosetti-Ferencei's insights into how Americans perceive Winston Churchill and in Richmond, Virginia to Ellen LeCompte for her resourcefulness and in her planning of the many events for the book's promotion in the USA.

I must also record my special gratitude to Randolph Churchill for his consistent enthusiasm for this project which I much value. We share a commitment to the English Speaking Union of which his great-grandfather was once chairman as much later was I. The English language so brilliantly deployed in Churchill's two orations at Fulton and Zurich was throughout his life his enabler, his platform, his sword.

I began preparing this book in a part of the world much loved by Winston Churchill, the Côte d'Azur. I wrote my first outline in the elegant and hospitable hotel La Réserve de Beaulieu, well known to Churchill, and I completed the first draft of the book in the same place. The incomparable beauty of the Côte inspired and comforted Churchill over many years as it has and does me.

Notes

Foreword

1 Celia Sandys, *Chasing Churchill: The Travels of Winston Churchill*, Unicorn Press, London, 2014, p. 100.
2 CAC, Churchill Papers, CHUR 2/158/46.

Chapter 1: The Warnings

1 Michael Walsh, *Witness to History*, Historical Review Press, 1996, p. 10.
2 Churchill responding to a toast by Stalin, Moscow, October 1944, in W. H. Thompson, *I Was Churchill's Shadow*, Christopher Johnson, London, 1959, p. 146.
3 Robert Rhodes James, *The Complete Speeches of Winston Churchill*, Chelsea House Publishers, London, 1974, p. 76.
4 Winston Churchill, *The Second World War*, Pimlico, London, 2002, p. 949.
5 Michael Dobbs, *Six Months in 1945: FDR, Stalin, Churchill, and Truman – From World War to Cold War*, Random House, London, 2013, p. 376
6 David Stahel, *Operation Typhoon*, Cambridge University Press, Cambridge, 2013, p. 6.
7 Robert Nisbet, *Roosevelt and Stalin: The Failed Courtship*, Regnery Gateway, Washington, DC, 1988, p. 103.
8 Conversation between the author and Sir Frank Roberts.
9 FCO, 'Britain and the Berlin Airlift', Information Pamphlet, HM Stationery Office, Innsworth, 1949, p. 12.
10 *Hansard*, debate 04 February 1948, vol. 446, cc.1811–4, 27 June 1948.

Chapter 2: Churchill and Roosevelt

1 Andrew Nagorski, *The Greatest Battle*, Simon & Schuster, New York, 2007, p. 132.
2 Nagorski, *The Greatest Battle*, p. 135.
3 Joseph Davies, *Mission to Moscow*, Garden City Publishing Company, New York, 1943, p. 172.
4 Alan Clark, *Barbarossa: The Russian–German Conflict*, William Morrow, New York, 1985, p. 407.
5 Robert Nisbet, *Roosevelt and Stalin: The Failed Courtship*, Regnery Gateway, Washington, DC, 1988, pp. 44–51.
6 Elliot Roosevelt, *As He Saw It*, Duell, Sloan and Pearce, New York, 1946.
7 *The Quotable Winston Churchill: A Collection of Wit and Wisdom*, Running Press, Philadelphia, p. 114.
8 Michael Jones, *After Hitler*, John Murray Publishers, London, 2015, p. 137.
9 Jones, *After Hitler*, p. 137.
10 Ibid.

Chapter 4: Genesis of the Journey

1 Letter of invitation by McCluer annotated by Truman, CAC, Churchill Papers, CHUR 2/230B/350.
2 Ibid.
3 Ibid.
4 *Hansard*, debate 12 November 1936, vol. 317, cc. 1081–155.
5 David Cannadine, *In Churchill's Shadow*, Penguin Books, London, 2001.
6 CAC, Churchill Papers, CHUR 5/4.
7 Mary Soames, *A Daughter's Tale*, Random House, London, 2011, p. 166.
8 Michael Dobbs, *Six Months in 1945: FDR, Stalin, Churchill, and Truman – From World War to Cold War*, Random House, London, 2013, p. 355.
9 Soames, *A Daughter's Tale*, p. 257.
10 Martin Gilbert, *In Search of Churchill*, HarperCollins, London, 1994, p. 364.

Chapter 5: 'I am deserted'

1 Lord Moran, *Churchill: The Struggle for Survival 1945–60*, Constable and Co., London, 1966, p. 314.

2 Winston Churchill, *My Early Life*, Touchstone, New York, 1958, p. 265.
3 Churchill Press Photographs, CHPH 12/F1/84.
4 Lord Moran, *Churchill*, p. 315.
5 CAC, Cadogan Papers, ACAD 1/13.
6 CAC, Cadogan Papers, ACAD 1/12.
7 CAC, Baroness Spencer-Churchill Papers, CSCT 1/24.
8 CAC, Attlee Papers, ATLE 2/2.
9 Ibid.
10 Ibid. For the full reply that Churchill never sent see CAC, Churchill Papers, CHUR 2/4/82.
11 Anthony Montague Browne, *Long Sunset*, Cassell, London, 1995, p. 112.
12 Winston S. Churchill, *Marlborough: His Life and Times, Book Two*, University of Chicago Press, Chicago, 2002, p. 1036.

Chapter 6: Outward Bound

1 Martin Gilbert, *Churchill: A Life*, Henry Holt and Company, New York, 1992, p. 862.
2 Winston Churchill, *Churchill by Himself*, Rosetta Books, London, 2013, p. 2.
3 Christopher H. Sterling, 'Churchill Afloat: The Liners He Rode', *Finest Hour*, Journal of the Churchill Centre and Societies, Winter 2003–2004, Number 121, p. 16.
4 Anthony Montague Browne, Long Sunset, Cassell, London, 1995, p. 74.
5 Lord Moran, *Churchill at War*, Constable and Co., London, 1996, pp. 20–21.
6 Michael Dobbs, *Six Months in 1945: FDR, Stalin, Churchill, and Truman – From World War to Cold War*, Random House, London, 2013, p. 45.
7 Dobbs, *Six Months in 1945*, p. 54.
8 Martin Gilbert, *Churchill and America*, Free Press, New York, 2005, p. 365.
9 Ibid., p. 364.

Chapter 7: Have a Holiday, Get a Loan

1 Winston Churchill, *My Early Life*, Touchstone, New York, 1958, p. 140.
2 CAC, Churchill Papers, CHAR 28/21/88.
3 CHPC 24, part 1.
4 CAC, Churchill Press Cuttings, CHPC 23, part 5.
5 CHPC 24, part 1.

6 William J. Bennett, *America: The Last Best Hope*, Thomas Nelson, Nashville, TN, 2007, p. 204.
7 Lord Moran, *Churchill: The Struggle for Survival 1940–65*, Constable & Co., London, p. 371.
8 Lord Moran, *Churchill at War*, Constable & Robinson, London, 1966, p. 371.

Chapter 8: A Synthesis of Agendas

1 Churchill responding to a toast by Stalin, Moscow, October 1944, in W. H. Thompson, *I Was Churchill's Shadow*, p. 146.
2 William Manchester, *The Last Lion: Winston Spencer Churchill: Visions of Glory, 1874–1932*, Michael Joseph Oxford 1983, p. 681
3 Ibid, p. 681.
4 Thomas Maier, *When the Lions Roar: The Churchills and the Kennedys*, Random House, New York, 2014, p. 430
5 Michael Dobbs, *Six Months in 1945: FDR, Stalin, Churchill, and Truman – From World War to Cold War*, Random House, London, 2013, p. 373.
6 George F. Kennan, *Memoirs 1925–1950*, Pantheon, New York, 1983, p. 35.
7 Ibid.

Chapter 9: Lord Halifax and the White House

1 David Reynolds, *In Command of History*, Penquin, London, 2005, p. 171.
2 Ibid.
3 CAC, Lady Onslow Papers, ONSL 1.
4 CAC, Churchill Press Cuttings, CHPC 23, part 6.
5 Ibid.
6 Ibid., part 5.

Chapter 10: The Train to Missouri

1 CAC, Lady Onslow Papers, ONSL 2.
2 Ibid.
3 Ibid.
4 CAC, CHU 34 2/4.
5 CAC, Lady Onslow Papers, ONSL 1.

6 Martin Gilbert, *Churchill: A Life*, Henry Holt and Company, New York, 1992, p. 869.
7 CAC, CHU 34 2/4.
8 Ibid.

Chapter 11: 'The most important speech of my life'

1 CAC, Lady Onslow Papers, ONSL 2.
2 Ibid.
3 Ibid.
4 CAC, Churchill Press Cuttings, CHPC 23, part 6.
5 CAC, Lady Onslow Papers, ONSL 2.
6 CHPC 24, part 1.
7 UMKC University Libraries, Kansas City, Broadcast #1, The War's Voices, Arthur B. Church, Marr Sound Archives.
8 CAC, Churchill Press Cuttings, CHPC 23.
9 CAC, CHUR 5/4A/51–100.
10 Ibid.
11 Ibid.
12 Ibid.

Chapter 12: Reactions I

1 CAC, Lady Onslow Papers, ONSL 2.
2 CAC, Churchill Press Cuttings, CHPC 23.
3 Roy Jenkins, *Churchill*, Macmillan, London, 2001, p. 811.
4 Frederick Winston Furneaux Smith, 2nd Earl of Birkenhead, *Life of Lord Halifax*, H. Hamilton, London, 1965, p. 458.
5 Andrew Roberts, *The Holy Fox: Biography of Lord Halifax*, Phoenix, London, 2004, p. 213.
6 David Reynolds, *In Command of History*, Penquin, London, 2005, p. 44.
7 Ibid., p. 201.
8 Graham Goodlad, 'Attlee, Bevin and Britain's Cold War', *History Review*, no. 69, 2011, pp. 1–6.
9 Ann and John Tusa, *The Berlin Blockade*, Hodder & Stoughton, London, 1988, p. 49.
10 CAC, CHUR 5/4A/51–100.
11 Ibid.
12 CAC, CHUR 5/4.

Chapter 13: With Ike to Richmond

1 CAC, CHU 34 2/4.
2 CAC, CHUR 5/4.
3 CAC, CHU 34 2/4.
4 John Bunyan, *The Pilgrim's Progress*, Wordsworth Classics, London, 1996, p. 243.
5 It was on this that Eisenhower responded afterwards suggesting an early meeting in the secretary of war's offices in Washington between Churchill and the US top military brass. It was to take place only a few days later with Churchill emphasising the 'intimacy of association' which had been the 'prevailing feature of our work together' in the war. Martin Gilbert, *Churchill and America*, Free Press, New York, 2005, p. 374.
6 CAC, Churchill Press Cuttings, CHU 54.
7 CAC, Churchill Press Cuttings, CHU 54.
8 CAC, Churchill Press Cuttings, CHPC 23.
9 CAC, Churchill Press Cuttings, CHPC 23.
10 Gilbert, *Churchill and America*, p. 323.

Chapter 14: Leaving the Big Apple

1 CAC, Churchill Press Cuttings, CHPC 23.
2 Ibid.
3 Roy Jenkins, *Churchill*, Macmillan, London, 2001, p. 706.
4 Ibid., p. 812.
5 Ibid.
6 Anne Applebaum, *Gulag: A History of Soviet Camps*, Penquin, London, 2004, p. xxiii.
7 Edvard Radzinsky, *Stalin: The 1st In-depth Biography Based on Explosive Documents from Russia's Secret Archives*, Anchor Books, New York, 1997, p. 499.
8 CAC, Churchill Press Cuttings, CHPC 23.
9 Ibid.
10 Ibid.
11 Ibid.
12 Ibid.
13 CAC, Churchill Papers, CHUR 5/4.
14 Barry Singer, *Churchill Style: The Art of Being Winston Churchill*, Abrams Image, New York, 2012, p. 121.
15 David Reynolds, *In Command of History: Churchill Fighting and Writing in the Second World War*, Penguin, London, 2005, p. 46.

Chapter 15: Homecoming

1 Martin Gilbert, *Churchill: A Life*, Henry Holt and Company, New York, 1992, p. 869.
2 David Reynolds, *In Command of History: Churchill Fighting and Writing in the Second World War*, Penguin, London, 2005, p. 47.
3 Hansard, debate 5 March 1946, vol. 420, cc. 193–294.
4 CAC, Churchill Press Cuttings, CHPC 23.
5 Deborah Cadbury, *Princes at War*, Bloomsbury Circus, London, 2015.
6 CAC, Churchill Press Cuttings, CHPC 23, part 5.
7 Warren Dockter, *Winston Churchill at the Telegraph*, Aurum Press, London, 2015, pp. 184–5.
8 David Reynolds, 'Marshall Plan Commemorative Section: The Marshall Plan Reconsidered: A Complex of Motives', *Foreign Affairs*, vol. 76, no. 3, 1997, p. 47.

Chapter 16: Zurich

1 CAC, Churchill Press Cuttings, CHPC 24, part 1, *Manchester Guardian*, 20 September 1946.
2 Ibid.
3 CAC, Churchill Papers, CHUR 5/8.

Chapter 17: Reactions II

1 CAC, Churchill Press Cuttings, CHPC 23.
2 Ibid.
3 Ibid.
4 Ibid.
5 Ibid.
6 Martin Gilbert *In Search of Churchill*, HarperCollins, London, 1994, p. 364.
7 Ibid., p. 731.
8 Robert Blake and William Roger Louis, *Churchill*, W. W. Norton and Company, New York, 1993, p. 491.
9 In the 1970s, when Britain eventually joined the European Common Market, I made an hour-long BBC television documentary about the Frenchman Jean Monnet known then as the 'Father of Europe', and who now has an honoured place in the Pantheon in Paris.

10 These are the words Monnet used when we spoke at his home in Houjarray.

11 Bradley W. Hart and Richard Carr, *The Foundations of the British Conservative Party*, Bloomsbury Academic, London, 2013, p. 312.

Chapter 18: The USA: From Irritation to Determination

1 Arthur Hugh Clough, 'Say Not the Struggle Naught Availeth', in *The Oxford Book of English Verse*, compiled by Arthur Thomas Quiller-Couch, Clarendon, Oxford, 1963.

2 Robert Blake and William Roger Louis, *Churchill*, W. W. Norton and Company, New York, 1993, p. 14.

3 Ann and John Tusa, Britain and the Berlin Airlift, RAF Air Historical Branch Stationery Office, Dd 9004493, p. 98, p. 5.

4 Simon Sebag Montefiore, *Stalin: The Court of the Red Tsar*, Orion, London, 2004, p. 442.

5 Ann and John Tusa, *The Berlin Blockade*, Hodder & Stoughton, 1988, p. 143.

6 Simon Sebag Montefiore, *Stalin* p. 488.

7 Anne Applebaum, *Gulag: A History of Soviet Camps*, Penquin, London, 2004, p. 467.

8 Forrest C. Pogue, *George C. Marshall*, Viking Press, New York, 1987, p. 193.

9 Ibid., p. 1963

10 Ibid.

11 President Truman's Message to Congress; March 12, 1947; Document 171; 80th Congress, 1st Session; Records of the United States House of Representatives; Record Group 233; National Archives.

12 Ibid.

13 Pogue, *George C. Marshall*, p. 164.

14 Ibid., p. 312.

15 Wilson D. Miscamble, *The Most Controversial Decision: Truman, the Atomic Bombs, and the Defeat of Japan*, Cambridge University Press, New York, 2011, p. 118.

Chapter 19: How and Why the Impact

1 Lord Moran, *Churchill: The Struggle for Survival 1945–60*, Constable and Co., London, 1966, p. 347.

2 CAC, Churchill Press Cuttings, CHPC 23.

3 Graham Farmelos, *Churchill's Bomb*, Faber and Faber, London, 2013, p. 145.

4 Richard Toye, *The Roar of the Lion: The Untold Story of Churchill's World War II Speeches*, Oxford University Press, Oxford, 2013, p. 59.

5 David Cannadine, Introduction, *The Speeches of Winston Churchill*, Penguin Books, New York, 1990, p. 85.

6 Ibid.

7 Ibid., p. 92.

8 Ibid.

9 Ibid., p. 93.

10 Ibid., p. 89.

11 Roy Jenkins, *Churchill*, Macmillan, London, 2001, p. 29.

12 Richard Holmes, *In the Footsteps of Churchill*, BBC Books, London, 2005, p. 40.

13 Ralph Martin, *Jennie: The Life of Lady Randolph Churchill*, Prentice Hall, Englewood Cliffs, NJ, 2008, p. 313.

14 Winston Churchill, *Thoughts and Adventures: Churchill Reflects on Spies, Cartoons, Flying, and the Future*, edited by James W. Muller, Paul. H. Courtenay and Alana L. Barton, ISI Books, Wilmington, DE, 2009.

15 Richard Holmes, *In the Footsteps of Churchill*, p. 40.

16 Martin Gilbert, *In Search of Churchill*, HarperCollins, London, 1994, p. 297.

17 Ibid., p. 298.

Chapter 20: Perspective

1 Roy Jenkins, *Churchill*, Macmillan, London, 2001, p. 37.

2 Isaiah Berlin, *Mr Churchill in 1940*, John Murray, London, 1949, p. 196.

3 Simon Sebag Montefiore, *Stalin: The Court of the Red Tsar*, Orion, London, 2004, p. 493.

4 Charles Mee, *Meeting at Potsdam*, M. Evans & Co., Maryland, 1975, p. 98.

5 Ibid., p. 104.

6 Martin Gilbert, *Churchill and America*, Free Press, New York, 2005, p. 401.

7 President Truman's Message to Congress; March 12, 1947; Document 171; 80th Congress, 1st Session; Records of the United States House of Representatives; Record Group 233; National Archives.

8 Ann and John Tusa, *The Berlin Blockade*, Hodder & Stoughton, London, 1988, p. 206.

9 Ibid., p. 576.

10 Roy Jenkins, *Truman*, Bloomsbury Reader, London, 2011, p. 270.

11 Philip Evanson, 'Churchill and the Sinews of Peace', *Georgia Review 1946–1955*, 1963, p. 237.
12 Ibid., p. 238.
13 Ibid., p. 237.
14 Ibid., p. 238.
15 Ashley Jackson, *Churchill*, Quercus, London, 2011, p. 150.

Letting Churchill Speak

1 See www.chu.cam.ac.uk/archives/
2 See www.churchillarchive.com.

Bibliography

Applebaum, Anne, *Gulag: A History of Soviet Camps*, Penguin, London, 2004

Bennett, William J., *America: The Last Best Hope*, Thomas Nelson, Nashville, TN, 2007

Berlin, Isaiah, *Mr Churchill in 1940*, John Murray Publishers, London, 1949

Blake, Robert and Roger Louis, William, *Churchill*, W. W. Norton and Company, New York, 1993

Browne, Anthony Montague, *Long Sunset*, Cassell, London, 1995

Bunyan, John, *The Pilgrim's Progress*, Wordsworth Classics, London, 1996

Cadbury, Deborah, *Princes at War*, Bloomsbury Circus, London, 2015

Cannadine, David, *The Speeches of Winston Churchill*, Penguin Books, New York, 1990

—, *In Churchill's Shadow*, Penguin Books, London, 2001

Cavendish, Richard, 'Farewell from the Commons', *History Today*, vol. 64, no. 7, July 2014

Churchill, Winston, *Churchill by Himself*, Rosetta Books, London, 2013

—, *Marlborough: His Life and Times Book Two*, University of Chicago Press, Chicago, 2002

—, *My Early Life*, Touchstone, New York, 1958

—, *The Second World War*, Pimlico, London, 2002

—, *Thoughts and Adventures: Churchill Reflects on Spies, Cartoons, Flying, and the Future*, ISI Books, Wilmington, DE, 2009

Clark, Alan, *Barbarossa: The Russian–German Conflict*, William Morrow, New York, 1985

Davies, Joseph, *Mission to Moscow*, Garden City Publishing Company, New York, 1943

Dobbs, Michael, *Six Months in 1945: FDR, Stalin, Churchill, and Truman – From World War to Cold War*, Random House, London, 2013

Dockter, Dr Warren, *Winston Churchill at the Telegraph*, Aurum Press, London, 2015

Evanson, Philip, 'Churchill and the Sinews of Peace', *Georgia Review 1946–1955*, 1963

Farmelos, Graham, *Churchill's Bomb*, Faber and Faber, London, 2013

Gilbert, Martin, *Churchill: A life*, Henry Holf & Co., New York, 1992, *Churchill and America*, Free Press, New York, 2005

—, *In Search of Churchill,* HarperCollins, London, 1994

Goodlad, Graham, 'Attlee, Bevin and Britain's Cold War', *History Review*, no. 69, 2011

Hart, Bradley W. and Richard Carr, *The Foundations of the British Conservative Party*, Bloomsbury Academic, London, 2013

Holmes, Richard, *In the Footsteps of Churchill*, BBC Books, London, 2005

Jackson, Ashley, *Churchill*, Quercus, London, 2011

Jenkins, Roy, *Truman*, Bloomsbury Reader, London, 2011

—, *Churchill*, Macmillan, London, 2001

Jones, Michael, *After Hitler*, John Murray Publishers, London, 2015

Kennan, George F., *Memoirs 1925–1950*, Pantheon, New York, 1983

Maier, Thomas, *When the Lions Roar: The Churchills and the Kennedys*, Random House, New York, 2014

Manchester, William, *The Last Lion: Winston Spencer Churchill: Visions of Glory, 1874–1932*, Michael Joseph, Oxford, 1983

Martin, Ralph, *Jennie: The Life of Lady Randolph Churchill*, Prentice Hall, Englewood Cliffs, NJ, 2008

Mee, Charles, *Meeting at Potsdam*, M. Evans & Co., Maryland, 1975

Miscamble, Wilson D., *The Most Controversial Decision: Truman, the Atomic Bombs, and the Defeat of Japan*, Cambridge University Press, New York, 2011

Moran, Lord, *Churchill: The Struggle for Survival 1945–60*, Constable and Co., London, 1966

—, *Churchill at War*, Constable & Robinson, London, 1966

Nagorski, Andrew, *The Greatest Battle*, Simon & Schuster, New York, 2007

Nisbet, Robert, *Roosevelt and Stalin: The Failed Courtship*, Regnery Gateway, Washington, DC, 1988

Pogue, Forrest C., *George C. Marshall*, Viking Press, New York, 1987

President Truman's Message to Congress; March 12, 1947; Document 171; 80th Congress, 1st Session; Records of the United States House of Representatives; Record Group 233; National Archives.

Quiller-Couch, Arthur Thomas, *The Oxford Book of English Verse*, Oxford University Press, Oxford, 1963

The Quotable Winston Churchill: A Collection of Wit and Wisdom, Running Press, Philadelphia, 2013

Radzinsky, Edvard, *Stalin: The 1st In-depth Biography based on Explosive Documents from Russia's Secret Archives*, Anchor Books, New York, 1997

Reynolds, David, *In Command of History: Churchill Fighting and Writing in the Second World War*, Penguin, London, 2005

—, 'Marshall Plan Commemorative Section: The Marshall Plan Reconsidered: A Complex of Motives', *Foreign Affairs*, vol. 76, no. 3, 1997

Rhodes James, Robert, *The Complete Speeches of Winston Churchill*, Chelsea House Publishers, London, 1974

Roberts, Andrew, *The Holy Fox: Biography of Lord Halifax*, Phoenix, London, 2004

Roosevelt, Elliot, *As He Saw It*, Duell, Sloan & Pearce, New York, 1946

Sandys, Celia, *Chasing Churchill: The Travels of Winston Churchill*, Unicorn Press, London, 2014

Sebag Montefiore, Simon, *Stalin: The Court of the Red Tsar*, Orion, London, 2004

Singer, Barry, *Churchill Style: The Art of Being Winston Churchill*, Abrams Image, New York, 2012

Smith, Frederick Winston Furneaux, 2nd Earl of Birkenhead, *The Life of Lord Halifax*, H. Hamilton, London, 1965

Soames, Mary, *A Daughter's Tale*, Black Swan, Random House, London, 2011

Stahel, David, *Operation Typhoon*, Cambridge University Press, Cambridge, 2013

Sterling, Christopher H., 'Churchill Afloat: The Liners He Rode', *Finest Hour*, Journal of the Churchill Centre and Societies, Winter 2003–2004, Number 121

Thompson, W. H., *I Was Churchill's Shadow*, Christopher Johnson, London, 1959

Toye, Richard, *The Roar of the Lion: The Untold Story of Churchill's World War II Speeches*, Oxford University Press, Oxford, 2013

Tusa, Ann and John, *The Berlin Blockade*, Hodder & Stoughton, London, 1988

—, 'Britain and the Berlin Airlift', RAF Air Historical Branch Stationery Office, Dd 9004493

UMKC University Libraries, Kansas City, Broadcast #1, The War's Voices, Arthur B. Church, Marr Sound Archives

Walsh, Michael, *Witness to History*, Historical Review Press, 1996

Index

A NOTE ON THE AUTHOR

Alan Watson is a broadcaster, author, High Steward of
Cambridge University, President of the Liberal Party, Public
Relations Consultant and Peer. An accomplished public speaker,
presenter, campaigner and consultant, his fascination with
Churchill has been lifelong. His enthusiasm for Britain at the
interface of Churchill's three circles – Europe, America, and the
English-speaking world – remains unmatched.

A NOTE ON THE TYPE

The text of this book is set in Bembo, which was first used in 1495 by the Venetian printer Aldus Manutius for Cardinal Bembo's *De Aetna*. The original types were cut for Manutius by Francesco Griffo. Bembo was one of the types used by Claude Garamond (1480–1561) as a model for his Romain de l'Université, and so it was a forerunner of what became the standard European type for the following two centuries. Its modern form follows the original types and was designed for Monotype in 1929.